RADICAL SERMONS FOR A RADICAL GENERATION

By Dana Kramer

All Scripture quotations unless otherwise indicated, are taken from the New King James Version®. Copyright © 1982 by Thomas Nelson, Inc. Used by permission. All rights reserved.

Other books by Dana Kramer:
    The Counterfeit Woman
    Slain Lamb Standing
    Random Thoughts For A Random Generation

2017 Dana Kramer

All rights reserved by the author. The author guarantees all contents are original and do not infringe upon the legal rights of any other person or work. No part of this book may be reproduced in any form without the permission of the author.

ISBN 978-0-6928-9400-2

Printed in the United State of America

TABLE OF CONTENTS

Introduction 5

Born of Water 7

Casual Christianity 16

Our Treasures Bring Darkness/Light 26

What's the Difference?. 32

The Marriage Supper of the Lamb. 41

The Voice of the Bridegroom 53

Calling Down Fire 62

Love Never Fails 69

Sincere, But Ignorant 76

Perdition 82

What Was God Thinking? 92

What Does the Last Days Outpouring Look Like?. 100

The Last Trumpet (Ever)! 106

God is in Complete Control at All Times! 114

INTRODUCTION

In this "new age" of Christianity, we are seeing many different faces beginning to appear. There is the face of easy born-again-ism that leads to a very watered down version of casual discipleship that pursues worldly treasures more than the heavenly. The Church doesn't take God at His word and makes up their own in order to obtain a feel-good faith. In turn, we hear proclamations such as "Don't judge me, Brother" or "Your not walking in love like Paul told us to." We have settled for a watered down version of God speaking to us, thus taking many Scriptures out of context in order to make Christianity easier. Below is a quote from Smith Wigglesworth:

> "The reason the world is not seeing Jesus is that Christian people are not filled with Jesus. They are satisfied with attending meetings weekly, reading the Bible occasionally, and praying sometimes. It is an awful thing for me to see people who profess to be Christians lifeless, powerless, and in a place where their lives are so parallel to unbelievers' lives that it is difficult to tell which place they are in, whether in the flesh or in the Spirit."[1]

In this generation, we are seeing waves of perversion, deception, defilement, and abomination, which also seem to be creeping into the Church stealthily on a daily basis. We are not seeing a Biblical standard raised up anymore. I'm addressing lawlessness and hoping to bring a little sanity back into the hearts and minds of those who have gone astray from the truth. If you respectfully receive God's grace, without cheapening it, and seek His face with sincerity to hear His voice then please disregard this book!

---

[1] http://www.azquotes.com/author/19437-Smith_Wigglesworth

BORN OF WATER???????

November 3, 2016

*"Unless one is born of **water** and the Spirit, he cannot enter the kingdom of God."* (John 3:5 – emphasis mine)

    I have always thought this verse was talking about water baptism, because Jesus was baptized so must we also be baptized. After searching the Scriptures, I began to see some truth emerge and that there's more concerning this mystery that Jesus had spoken of to Nicodemus. In the next few paragraphs, I will present some of my findings from Scripture on this subject. Although these truths will not be all conclusive, they will present, what I believe, is the definition of being born again. If we get our birth into God's kingdom wrong, then our life will be in error continuously.

    I have heard someone define Jesus' statement in John 3:8,

> *"The wind blows where it wishes . . . so is everyone who is born of the Spirit."*

This was their definition: Whoever is born again just follows the Spirit and you never know where the Spirit will take you and no one else will know either. Is this what Jesus was saying? Jesus was speaking this in context of being born of **water** and the Spirit. He was saying you could hear the wind when it blows; so also you can hear water when it flows. Let me explain. Jeremiah 10:13 and 51:16 both say the same,

> *"When He utters His voice, there is a multitude of **waters** in the heavens."* (Jeremiah 10:13 - emphasis mine)

This is either the sound of people responding to His voice or it is what His voice sounds like. The utterance of God's voice is likened to the sound of a multitude of waters. In the same two verses the Scripture also speaks of the wind coming out of His treasuries.

> *"He brings the wind out of His treasuries."*
> (Jeremiah 51:16)

We know that wind is a symbol of the Holy Spirit, but what is water a symbol of? Most believers only get caught up on the wind and moving of the Holy Spirit (dreams, visions, etc.) Living water is His voice speaking that will bring change in someone's life in an instant; where programs,. meetings, and small groups could take years. I'm only emphasizing the importance of individually hearing and receiving God's voice.

Jesus again speaks of water when He has an encounter with the woman at the well. He says to her,

> *"If you knew the gift of God, and who it is who says to you, 'Give Me a drink,' you would have asked Him, and He would have given you living water."*
> (John 4:10)

He then tells her that this water will become a fountain within her springing up to eternal life. The water that Jesus gives her is His very words! This is better explained in Revelation 1:15 as John describes;

> *" . . . and **His voice as the sound of many waters**."*
> (emphasis mine)

Revelation 14:2 speaks the same thing;

> *"I heard a voice from heaven, **like the voice of many waters**."* (emphasis mine)

In every believer who hears God, there will come a fountain of God's words springing up and leading to eternal life; just as Romans 10:10 says,

> *"For with the heart one believes unto righteousness, and with the mouth confession is made unto salvation."*

The woman at the well simply believed His words and was changed in an instant. Believing His words in our heart will ALWAYS result in a fountain of His words coming out of our mouth! It can never be any other way! When God, through His Word, takes up residence in someone's heart the results will always be God's words coming out of our mouth. I ask myself many times who it is who lives in me, because I speak so many things that don't pertain to God's heart and interests. Jesus is so much like His Father and we see that comparison in Ezekiel's book. Ezekiel 1:24 explains:

> *"When they* (the living creatures) *went, I heard the noise of their wings, **like the noise of many waters, like the voice of the Almighty**!"* (emphasis mine)

The voice of Jesus and the voice of the Almighty sound exactly the same; like the sound of many waters! We know this to be true because Jesus told His disciples that He only speaks what He hears the Father saying. The Holy Spirit also only speaks what the Father speaks as is written in John 16:14. Jesus says,

> *"All things that the Father has are Mine. Therefore I said that He will take of Mine and declare it to you."*

We will notice in John 7:38 that Jesus cries out on the last day of the feast these very words;

> *"He who believes in Me . . . out of his heart will flow rivers of living water."*

John explains that Jesus was speaking of the Holy Spirit. When the day of Pentecost came, what was the result of being filled with the Holy Spirit? They spoke! They didn't just speak unintelligible words, they spoke in many languages expounding on God's workings and all understood what they said. Were they saying things like, "I can feel His presence" or "God is right here with us"? Yes! But is that all they were saying? I believe they were speaking the very word of God to each other. The word of God coming straight from the OLD TESTAMENT! There wasn't a New Testament yet. Remember in Jeremiah 10:13 and 51:16 there being two things mentioned: His voice uttered, and bringing the wind out of His treasuries. On the day of Pentecost God brought out the Wind from His treasury and began speaking directly into their hearts. His word and the Holy Spirit can never be separated! When you feel His presence, He is also, at that very moment in anticipation, wanting to speak His Word with His Voice into our hearts! You can't feel His presence without hearing what He has to say! Peter told Jesus not to wash his feet. Jesus told Peter,

> *"If I do not wash you, you have no part with Me."*
> (John13:8)

Was it just washing Peter's feet that made the difference? In response to Jesus' words, Peter wanted more than his feet washed. Jesus again told him,

> *"Anyone who has bathed needs only to wash his feet, but is clean all over. And you [My disciples] are clean."* (John 13:10 - AMP)

How had they become clean? As Paul says in Ephesians 5:26, they were clean through the washing of water by the word. Paul connects water with the word. Paul also says in I Corinthians 6:9-11, that some who had received Jesus used to be fornicators, homosexuals, covetous, foulmouthed revilers, thieves and drunkards, but had been washed. Jesus told His disciples in John 15:3

> *"You are already clean because of the word which I have spoken to you."*

All that being said, how has being born again made a difference in our lives? Is it that we only look backwards to the day God saved us or are we to be consistently saved through the washing of His voice speaking to us!? Water baptism is a sign of being completely immersed and washed in God's voice of words! Again, I must ask, if we don't spend time in worship and His word, how can He speak to us? It's all about relationship! Is Sunday morning enough time for this? Is Sunday morning plus an hour of daily devotions enough time to establish relationship with God? Ask your spouse or friend if that is enough time for a deep meaningful relationship to become established!

In Mark 4:20-25, the parable of the sower, Jesus says that those who hear the word and accept it, bear fruit thirty, sixty, and one hundred fold. The emphasis is not on the percentage amount of fruit that we have, but on the hearing of the word that leads to a lamp being lit up! Is your lamp lit? It's not a matter of hiding your lit up lamp or not. It's hearing and receiving Jesus' words that lights up our lamp! Jesus says in Mark 4:24,

> *"To you who hear, more will be given."*

Those who listen will experience an ever-increasing dialog between you and the Father. This is the meaning of the parable of the ten virgins. The five foolish didn't have an on going relationship so they lacked enough oil to keep their lamps lit when the Bridegroom came. The five wise virgins had enough oil because of on going relationship. Their lamps were lit through hearing His voice consistently! This is relationship! We know Him because we listen and hear Him! Notice what one of the elders in Revelation 7 says to John concerning those who come out of the tribulation and serve God in His temple.

> *"The Lamb who is in the midst of the throne will shepherd them and lead them to living fountains of waters* (Revelation 7:17)

This is a picture of living in and consistently drinking in of God's voice through the power of the Holy Spirit! Again Revelation 22:1 and 17 sum up what I've been saying,

> *"He showed me a pure river of water of life, clear as crystal, proceeding from the throne of God and of the Lamb!"*

They don't have to speak a thing. Their words, like a river, emanate from their very being; without flaw or any contamination of evil! Words speaking volumes without even saying a thing! Words that light up the entire universe! Words that flood our very beings with resplendent light!

> *"Whoever desires, let him take the water of life freely!"*

This is what it means to be born again of water and the Spirit! Blessings!

THIS IS WHAT THE LAST DAYS OUTPOURING WILL LOOK LIKE:

The diligent, ravenous, undeterred seeking of truth in and through the Words of God written in His book and not hit and miss prophecies or the absorption of lukewarm, leftover sermons handed down from decades gone by!

CASUAL CHRISTIANITY
November 5, 2016

      There have been many times I have been sitting in a church service or even in a prayer room worshipping the Lord and a thought will hit me out of the blue demanding my attention. I become somewhat overwhelmed by this thought because it completely separates the reality I'm experiencing from the true and eminent reality that is to come. This would be true even if the reality that is to come were to manifest in a millisecond or 100 years from now. As I'm in worship and caught up in the presence of God, I will open my eyes and look around to see others worshipping the Lord as well. As I look around at various people, I see some with hands raised to heaven. I also see some rocking back and forth as they worship. Others stand there in what seems to be a motionless stance before the Lord. It is at these times that I wonder to myself what they see as they worship? Why do some seem so relaxed as if they don't have a care in the world, while others are just looking around as if completely distracted by people and surroundings? I wonder, what are they focused on? I see some dancing and jumping, some on their knees with their hands raised, some giving proclamations of faith and proclaiming Scripture, and then there are others sitting quietly looking as if they could almost be asleep. One thing that seems to be missing most often is tears. Tears can mean sorrow, regret, or an overwhelming experience; like unexplainable joy mixed with the terror of the Lord. When I say terror, I'm not talking about the experience that causes someone's hair to stand on end and be afraid. I'm talking about an experience that is so far beyond your comprehension that you have a major shutdown in the heart; being overwhelmed to the point of almost being comatose. This is what John experienced when He saw Jesus as described in Revelation 1:17:

"And when I saw Him, I fell at His feet as dead."

This thought that comes to my mind overwhelms me and it causes me to have this same response. I don't stop worshipping, but my response to the Lord changes and my attitude definitely is different. I become focused immediately. These questions also happen at other times outside the church when I'm with or around other believers just doing everyday life. I'm then struck with this same reality of mind that again sobers me up instantly. You're probably wondering what these thoughts are that I have; (and no, it doesn't have anything to do with a rapture).

    I've observed many a Christian looking at their e-mail or texting during a time of worship. Sometimes I see a brother greeting another brother during worship and the conversation is several minutes long. Some have even been doing homework during worship. I'm not presenting these things because I have a critical spirit. Please don't misunderstand what I am saying. I see these things as the results of "Casual Christianity". We live in a society where fun, food, and frolic are pursued with blind aggression. What I mean is that these things are hotly pursued, but with no conscious restraint. It's almost as if we have the attitude that God gave them to us so we can't live without them. We have been taught this paradigm since we were kids. Recently I heard a commercial regarding a certain vacation destination. It proudly claims that happiness is around every corner. Does this sound like heaven or should this be considered false advertising? There are times I take my wife out to a restaurant and I will sit and observe the casualness of individuals enjoying a fine meal. Don't misunderstand, we all need times of refreshing and we also need time with our loved ones. What I am addressing is that this activity becomes the norm and we must have it in order to be happy. This reminds me of a Scripture verse in Ezekiel 16:49 (AMP),

> *"Behold, this was the iniquity of your sister Sodom: pride, overabundance of food, prosperous ease, and idleness."*

If I wasn't mistaken, I would think this verse was talking about America. With the mention of food in abundance, next time you are out and about, try counting all the restaurants that you pass by. Better yet, maybe it would be easier to count the restaurants in the phone book. Within greater Kansas City there is estimated 1,780 eateries. Out of these are 88 Subways, 61 McDonalds, and 42 Taco Bells; not to mention KFC's, Burger Kings, Arby's, Wendy's and the greasy spoon down the street (lol). It seems that a person just blinks and a new restaurant is being built. This would not include the massive grocery markets such as Wal-mart, Target, and hundreds of others. Did Jesus see this time we are living in when He said,

> *"As it was in the days of Lot so will it be in the days of the Son of Man, they were eating and drinking"*
> (Luke 17:28).

I don't believe Sodom was inundated with restaurants, so Jesus wasn't referring to being in an eatery. He was referring to the Sodomites casually ignoring Lot's preaching. Genesis 19:1 says that Lot used to sit at the gate. That was where the elders of the city would sit and counsel the people. He must have been trying to reform the Sodomites because in Genesis 19:9, they accused him of acting like a judge. They apparently did not like what he was saying. If you remember, Lot had a very hot message after his encounter with the two angels: God is going to destroy this place so get out of Sodom now! Yet they were fixed on enjoying fun, food, and frolic. No worries whatsoever!

This Casual Christianity takes on several forms in this day and age. The extreme love of music and the many genres that we have to choose from is also one of them. We choose our music as if we are choosing an entree' at a steakhouse. Is it tender, or does it have to have a little aggression. Music was my life before salvation. I listened to the Rolling Stones, Black Oak Arkansas, Alice Cooper and Ozzie. I had to have "fire" in the music I listened to. When I became a believer I didn't change my music genre, I just changed the artists. I was still a head-banger at heart; only a Casual Christian head-banger. I still acted like a heathen, yet I had given Someone entrance into my life and He begin to take over! Little did I know at the time that He was going to eventually consume my whole life like a lion would consume his prey. Oh, did I mention that He is called the Lion of the Tribe of Judah (and His name isn't Aslan)! I believe God hates Casual Christianity! I don't see this lifestyle in the Bible, especially in the Hebrews hall of fame (chapter 11). The Lord likens Himself in Scripture many times to a lion. Lions are not majestically cute and cuddly! They are not casual about their decisions! They devour!

So what is this thought that comes to mind? I preface my answer with a Scripture. Revelation 6:15-16,

> *"The kings of the earth, the great men, the rich men, the commanders, the mighty men, every slave and every free man, hid themselves in the caves and in the rocks of the mountains, and said to the mountains and rocks, 'Fall on us and hide us from **the face of Him who sits on the throne**."* (emphasis mine)

What is it about His face that scares these people to death? And why are they running and hiding?

I believe His face will rock our "Casual Christianity" world as well as the unsaved. First we will look at those who almost saw His face. Exodus 19 describes Israel's encounter with the Lord. Mount Sinai was on fire, and smoke covered its surface. The mountain shook as thunder and lightning exploded in the sky. There was also the sound of a trumpet blast that seemed to increase in volume. The Lord came down on the mountain and called Moses to Himself. All of a sudden the Lord is telling Moses to go down and warn the people not to break through the smoke and haze to gaze at the Lord. If they were to see Him they would have instantly died, because He would have broke out against them. I'm not sure what it means to break out against them, but it doesn't sound good. Israel had rebelled and rejected God's leading many times so I can only assume they were not prepared for what they would see and encounter.

A few chapters later in Exodus 24 we see Moses, Aaron, his sons, plus 70 elders going up on the mountain again. This time they saw God who had under His feet the work of clear paved sapphire stone. It does say they saw God, or as Amplified puts it,

> *"[A convincing manifestation of His presence]."*

If you were to see God (or a manifestation of His presence) what would your response be? It says their response was

> *"They saw God, and **they ate and drank**."* (emphasis mine)

Keep in mind they had already experienced Mount Sinai on fire with thunder, lightning and ever increasing trumpet blasts. God overlooked their casualness, because it says in verse 11 AMP,

> *"He laid not His hand [to conceal Himself from them, to rebuke their daring, or to harm them]."*

After a terrifying experience with God on a burning mountain, it would seem that any casualness would not be a factor. A note on Aaron's two sons, Nadab and Abihu who, later in Leviticus 10 casually offered strange fire to God and were burned up. This probably put the fear of God in Aaron and his other two sons.

Moses asks to see God's glory. God responds and says to him,

> *"I will make all My goodness pass before you . . .* ***but you cannot see My face; for no man shall see Me and live."*** (emphasis mine)

There is something about that face! The list of men, in Revelation 6, are terrified to see His face. Moses had to be terrified of seeing God's face and rightly so, just as it says in Revelation 20:11,

> *"I saw a great white throne and Him who sat on it,* ***from whose face the earth and the heaven fled away."*** (emphasis mine)

If earth and heaven flee in terror why are we so casual? Yes, we can be at peace and not be terrified because Jesus loves us! But I'm afraid there has come casualness in the knowledge of this truth and we have dulled down the truth about the fear of the Lord! I've got one more example. John describes his experience with seeing Jesus' face.

> ***"When I saw Him, I fell at His feet as dead."***
> (emphasis mine)

Why would someone who had walked with Jesus three and one-half years knowing how much He was loved by Him, fall down almost dead before Him? John only saw Jesus' face and this was his response! Why do the 24 elders fall down on their faces every time His name is mentioned? What do these men see that we don't? Will our casualness become a detriment when we stand before Him and look into His face? We can only have true fellowship with each other if we walk in light as Jesus walked in light. God is light! John saw Jesus' face shining brighter than the sun because Jesus, being a man, had the fullness of God dwelling within Him. So if God is resplendent light and He dwells in Jesus and John fell as a dead man before Jesus, what happens when we gaze into the face of Him who sits on the throne? We who are servants and love God extremely can take comfort in Revelation 22:4.

"There shall be no more curse, but the throne of God and of the Lamb shall be in it, and His servants shall serve Him. **They shall see His face, and His name shall be on their foreheads.*"*** (emphasis mine)

So, in describing all the thoughts that I have in those moments, this is the main question: **In all of our times of worship and service to the Lord, do we worship and speak to Him as if we are looking directly into His face?** I can boldly say that this would change our casual way of living and worship. He's not out to kill us, but to devour our entire being with His loving Face!

THIS IS WHAT THE LAST DAYS OUTPOURING WILL LOOK LIKE:

"Hear me, O Lord, hear me, that this people may know that You are the Lord God. Then **the fire of the Lord fell** and consumed the burnt sacrifice, the wood, stones, dust and water. When all the people saw it, **they fell on their faces**!" (I Kings 18:37-39 – emphasis mine)

Zeal for the Lord's people consumed Elijah and moved him to obey the Lord in a most radical form. His obedience put him in a very precarious situation and failure of God responding would have cost him his life. God loved his passion! The fire fell and then the people fell!

OUR TREASURES BRING DARKNESS/LIGHT

November 11, 2016

Below I am writing out the following verses from Matthew 6:19-24 as I have perceived them. A verse or two has been skipped in between, but you should be able to see the picture that Jesus was presenting.

> *"Do not lay up for yourselves **treasures on earth** . . . For where your treasure is, **there your heart will be** also. The lamp of the body is the eye . . . if therefore your **eye is bad,** your whole body will be **full of darkness** . . . No one can serve two masters."*
> (emphasis mine)

Jesus just said your heart and your eye are one and the same, equating the laying up of earthly treasure with darkness. If your eye is on earthly things then your heart will also be full of darkness. He then says no one can serve two masters, or no one can have his eye on two treasures at the same time.

Now let's look at Matthew 6:20-24 from a different light.

> *"Lay up for yourselves **treasures in heaven**...for where your treasure is, **there your heart will be** also. The lamp of the body is the eye. If therefore your **eye is good**, your whole body will be **full of light**...No one can serve two masters."* (emphasis mine)

Jesus is equating treasures stored in heaven with light. If your eye is on heavenly things, your heart is full of light. Jesus also gives us warning in Luke 11:35 regarding this same topic:

> *"Therefore take heed that the light which is in you is not darkness."*

Matthew 6:23 says it this way:

> *"If therefore the light that is in you is darkness, how great is that darkness!"*

Jesus is saying that earthly treasures can be very deceptive if we equate them with God's blessing (light). If this light (earthly treasures to enjoy) is darkness and we are only focused on earthly things to get pleasure from, how great is that darkness. In other words, we believe God blesses us because of the good life that we have here on earth. We have made the good life (THE AMERICAN DREAM) our light, which is great darkness.

Consider Jesus: What treasures was He focused on? We must conclude that He was only focused on the heavenly or eternal because of the light that was in Him. He had been focused on the eternal since He was a young child growing up into manhood. On the day He was baptized by John, the heavens opened and God spoke,

> *"This is My beloved Son, in whom I am well pleased!"*

God's light now flooded over Jesus at His baptism. When He was transfigured before Peter, James, and John, His face shone like the sun and His clothes became white as light. Again God spoke audibly. Jesus' focus was on God only and that was the result! Look again at Revelation 1:14,16; 19:12 and 21:23.

> *"His eyes like a flame of fire . . . and His countenance was like the sun shining in its strength."*
>
> *"His eyes were like a flame of fire."*
>
> *"The city had no need of the sun or of the moon to shine in it, for the glory of God illuminated it. The Lamb is its light."*

Because Jesus emptied Himself in order to allow God and His glory to be His treasure, He became the light of the city New Jerusalem. Revelation 22:5 says that there will be no night in the New Jerusalem because God's glory within Jesus lights it up. This verse also speaks of God's servants who serve Him:

> *"They need no lamp nor light of the sun, for the Lord gives them light. They shall reign forever and ever."*

They will reign forever with Jesus because they made their treasure in heaven allowing God's light to flood their lives. As Jesus said:

> *"You are the light of the world, a city set on a hill!"*

We have no idea what God has in store for those who make Him their treasure. He who overcomes will inherit all things! Please, if you know what "all things" means, let me know of your discovery. I would very much like to hear it.

THIS IS WHAT THE LAST DAYS OUTPOURING LOOKS LIKE:

"Daniel interpreted Nebuchadnezzar's dream . . .
Then King Nebuchadnezzar fell on his face!"
(Daniel 2:24-46 – emphasis mine)

What does it look like for a person to relate to a wicked king who has just destroyed your place of worship, your home and your city, who has killed some of your relatives and enslaved the rest, and made you a castrated single who will never marry? What does it look like for a king to be overcome by the presence of God and fall on his face before the one whom he did all of this to? Kings will fall on their face before the Lord as He pours out His Spirit without measure in the last days! We, like Daniel, must walk without offense before our Nebuchadnezzar. He will fall on his face!

WHAT'S THE DIFFERENCE?
November 11, 2016

Paul gives two lists of evil men; one in Romans and one in II Timothy. There is a marked difference between the two!

1. Romans 1:28-31: *"God gave them over to a debased mind... being filled with all unrighteousness, sexual immorality, wickedness, covetousness, maliciousness; full of envy, murder, strife, deceit, evil-mindedness; they are whisperers, backbiters, haters of God, violent, proud, boasters, inventors of evil things, disobedient to parents, undiscerning, untrustworthy, unloving, unforgiving, unmerciful."*
2. 2 Timothy 3:1-5: *"But know this, that in the last days perilous times will come: For men will be lovers of themselves, lovers of money, boasters, proud, blasphemers, disobedient to parents, unthankful, unholy, unloving, unforgiving, slanderers, without self-control, brutal, despisers of good, traitors, headstrong, haughty, lovers of pleasure rather than lovers of God, having a form of godliness but denying its power."*

First we will look at the list in Romans. The people described in Romans 1 have suppressed or ignored the truth since the creation of the world. They had seen God clearly through all of His creation, but chose to reject it. So in turn, became foolish and were filled with darkness. They then looked to the created things to represent their god. This became a spiral downward towards lusts of various kinds dishonoring their bodies among themselves. We see this as far back in Scripture as Genesis 6 when men lusted, under the power of the demonic, towards women who were under the power of the demonic, having presented themselves as sexually beautiful. God said He was sorry that He had made man because man's heart had become continually evil. These had been given over to a debased mind just as Paul has described. We also see this rejection of the truth in Genesis 19 as described by Moses concerning Sodom and their depravity. So from the beginning of creation all the way up to the time of the Roman Empire, we see those who have rejected the truth given over to a debased mind. Time after time there is described in Scripture the evil deeds that were done by mankind because they rejected the truth. But a change is about to happen!

A deliverer was to be born who would save the people from their sin. I am so glad that Jesus saved me from a life of evil and from a reprobate mind. Those living in the time of the Roman Empire also received this tremendous gift from God. Their hearts were transformed and their minds were cleansed. It was the blood of the sacrifice of the One who hung on a tree; becoming a curse for mankind that washed them clean forever! The Church was born, that beautiful city that is described in Revelation 21 and 22. Man would never be the same because of this Holy Man from heaven. We have seen the Church advance for over 2000 years. She has become a force for change throughout the entire world. Holy Spirit has given her the power to see many swept into the kingdom throughout history of which many of us today have become partakers of this miracle. It's no wonder that Revelation 7:9 says that John saw a great multitude which could not be numbered standing in heaven proclaiming with loud voices their love for God. We will see the fruit of our labors when Jesus comes back and rewards those who have been faithful in their love and service. I long for this day to come!

Jesus gave us a warning though through one of the parables. After He shares the parable of the wheat and tares, which describes good seed and bad seed, He says something very disheartening:

> *"Let both grow together until the harvest"* (Matthew 13:30)

The bad seed has to grow with the good seed? Why? Have you ever asked this question? Needless to say there are many reasons given as to why this is allowed, but that's for another time.

Let's now turn our attention to II Timothy 3 and the second list that Paul has given. This list is so similar to the one in Romans that one would think they are both talking about the same group of people. They are both describing very similar sins, yet the people in these two groups are different. In the Scriptures leading up to the list mentioned in II Timothy 3, we see Paul mentions two men: Hymenaeus and Philetus. He says these men have strayed from the truth, yet their message will spread like cancer. So when Paul mentions these men he is warning those in the faith to avoid them because they have strayed from the truth. Paul continues by describing a great house and that the vessels found in this house would be made of gold and silver, yet there would also be vessels of wood and clay; vessels for honor and dishonor. With this in mind Paul warns God's people:

> *"But know this, that in the last days perilous times will come!"*

He is warning those in the church that there will be people claiming the name of Jesus, yet will be lovers of themselves, lovers of money, etc. Those listed in Romans 1 didn't see or have the opportunity to receive Jesus so they just gave themselves over to evil. These mentioned in II Timothy have tasted the Lord's goodness in Jesus. They come to church and even present themselves as dedicated believers, yet their heart is corrupted. Now if you have a sensitive heart, you will probably say (like myself) "This describes my life at times!" Don't be disheartened! God knows your heart and He keeps it very close to His own. The only reason I mention these things is because of the deception that will increasingly arise in the last days. These people listed in II Timothy 3 are in contrast to those who desire to live a godly life and search daily the Holy Scriptures, which make us wise to the devil's schemes. If we see something in our heart that is corrupt, we must immerse ourselves in His Word because

> *"All Scripture is given by inspiration of God, and is profitable for doctrine, for reproof, for correction, for instruction in righteousness, that the man of God may be complete, thoroughly equipped for every good work"* (II Timothy 3:16-17).

As Psalms 119:9 AMP says,

> *"How shall a young man cleanse his way? By taking heed and keeping watch [on himself] according to Your word [conforming his life to it]."*

The deception that will come in the last days has already begun and will only get more intense. In mentioning the parable of the wheat and tares, the amplified bible replaces the word "tares" with the word "darnel" which is a weed that closely resembles wheat. In these days that we live, there have been so many preachers, teachers, and prophets emerge all proclaiming that they have the word of the Lord. I'm not about pointing a finger at people, but I am about believers studying to show themselves approved and being wise as serpents in this day and age we live in. We must know what God says in His word --- OLD AND NEW Testament. We also must be filled with the Holy Spirit of God, being ever so careful not to grieve Him by our disobedience. Wisdom still cries out in the streets as Proverbs proclaims. But I see many today crying out and even spewing out lies and false truths in order to desecrate the upright! I see this in the news media (liberal and conservative) and I also see it very prevalent on "social" media! There is no fear of God anymore! The fear of the Lord is the beginning of wisdom! We are entering into perilous times like no other time in history and we must give ourselves fully and completely to God. Jesus took on the form of a servant even though He was God in the flesh. We must follow

His example closely. He has extended mercy and grace to many people over and over, even when they have rejected Him. We must do the same. He forgave those who rejected, persecuted, and then killed Him. We must do the same. When we believe His word, a light comes on within us and it shines out for all to see. This crucified, resurrected Jesus life in us is the light that shines out to men. The darkness will get darker, BUT as this darkness flourishes it will appear as light! So many times I have said to myself, "I will recognize the darkness of the last days because it will be so evident." I'm not so sure about this now. Jesus says in Matthew 24:24,

> *"False christs and false prophets will rise and show great signs and wonders **to deceive, if possible, even the elect.**"* (emphasis mine)

False christs are not people running around claiming to be Jesus Christ. Because Christ means anointed one, they are supposedly anointed people who are preaching, teaching, or prophesying in His name. Jesus did say this would be a sign of the last days in Matthew 7:22-23.

> *"Many will say to Me in that day, 'Lord, Lord, have we not prophesied in Your name?'"*

Jesus answers with a very haunting word:

> *"I never knew you, depart from Me, you who practice lawlessness!"*

I believe the key to not being deceived is obedience! If one practices lawlessness, then there is no obedience since there is no law. If there is no law in a person's life, it's because they choose to ignore the law or they are completely ignorant of it as they choose to ignore His word by not reading it. Let's go into these last days full of wisdom and courage, knowing that the Captain of our faith has gone through everything we have experienced and has overcome. He also says to us,

> *"To him who overcomes I will grant to sit with Me on My throne, as I also overcame and sat down with My Father on His throne"* (Revelation 3:21)

Let me ask you a question: Does Jesus lie? Does He even exaggerate? If your answer is "no," then we've got to believe that what He says will come to pass! David was an overcomer and his name is mentioned by many prophets throughout the entire Bible in regards to ruling and reigning with Christ forever. In this; we see just a glimpse of God as a rewarder of those who walk in faith.

THIS IS WHAT THE LAST DAYS OUTPOURING LOOKS LIKE:

"And **one cried** to another **and said**: '**Holy**, holy, holy is the Lord of hosts; the whole earth is full of His glory!' And the posts of the door were shaken by the voice . . . **So I said: 'Woe is me, for I am undone!'**"
(Isaiah 6:3-5 – emphasis mine)

Isaiah was ok with just speaking for God until he had a vision of God's holiness and how breathtakingly magnificent, awesome, and wonderful the Lord was in His temple! He heard a voice violently shaking the posts and immediately saw his wretchedness! He became completely undone!

THE MARRIAGE SUPPER OF THE LAMB
(what does it look like?)

November 25, 2016

*"Let us be glad and rejoice and give Him glory, for the **marriage of the Lamb** has come, and His wife has made herself ready."*
*"Blessed are those who are called to the **marriage supper of the Lamb**!"* (Revelation 19:7,9 – emphasis mine)

    In the next few paragraphs I will endeavor to paint a picture of what I believe is the description and portrayal of the marriage (or marriage supper) of the Lamb. Most of my saved life I have pictured this event as portrayed several years ago by someone's photograph of an extremely long table; set with many, many settings of fine china, crystal, and golden dinnerware. The table went on into infinity; which captured your imagination. I always questioned this portrayal because it was so much like what we do here on earth. Jesus taught us to pray that what was in heaven would come to earth, so the marriage supper portrayed in that picture seemed so earthly and fleshly, and without much intimate fellowship with Jesus just by the magnitude of it. Please stay with me on this and I think you will see why I have changed my views on this subject. Again, please study for yourself to see if I'm right.

In any marriage there has to be a bride and a bridegroom. They must be in love with each other for this event to take place. We know that Jesus is our Bridegroom. He has shown us His love for us by laying down His life and being crucified on a tree. As Deuteronomy 21:23 says,

"He who is hanged (on a tree) *is accursed of God."*

He took the curse for us! This is love! So, what do we do with this kind of love? As a bride, we respond with love in return. Yet sometimes our love for Him seems so tainted and defiled with other desires. He already knows this, yet loves us anyway. As Misty Edwards sings in one of her songs:

> "I knew what I was getting into when I called you.
> I knew what I was getting into when I said your name, but I said it just the same.
> And I am not shocked by your weakness.
> And I am not shocked even by your sin.
> And I am not shocked by your brokenness.
> I knew what I was getting into and I still want you.
> I knew what I was getting into and I still like you.
> I knew what I was getting into and I still chose you."

This song humbles me every time I hear it. My vain thoughts say if He were to know me (really know me), would He still love me? Truth is, He already knew me even before I knew Him! We know what we are like on the inside and we try to hide these things from everyone else, including God. We are locked up, screwed up, and messed up, but He still loves us! So what do we make of the Scripture that says in Revelation 19:7,

"His wife has made herself ready"?

My wife made herself ready for me by looking very beautiful on our wedding day. But it was much more than that! Her heart was set on me as her only lover and friend. Was she perfect? The answer to this will be our little secret. If our love is perfect, then why do we need someone to test it? Love is always tested by the one you love! God made it this way. Point being; we see and know that our love is imperfect. How do we make our selves ready to be His bride?

THE FRIEND OF THE BRIDEGROOM

One of the ways we become ready is through the friends of the bridegroom. John labeled himself a friend of the bridegroom in John 3:29,

> *"He who has the bride is the bridegroom; but the friend of the bridegroom, who stands and hears him, rejoices greatly because of the bridegroom's voice."*

John was a special messenger sent to prepare hearts for the coming of the Messiah. He was also the bride, yet took the position of friend of the bridegroom. This was a love relationship as well. The friend desires the best for the groom and we see this played out in John the Baptist. His only desire was to see the groom made very desirable to the bride. John didn't just baptize and tell people how much Jesus loved them. He spoke very firmly about getting right with God and turning from an evil heart. Some of John's vocabulary was very strong. He called the religious leaders who were coming to His baptisms a "brood of vipers!" He said things like

> *"The axe is laid to the root of the trees. Therefore every tree which does not bear good fruit is cut down and thrown into the fire."*

These do not seem like words that would endear a bride, yet John knew the heart of this people. They were far from the Lord. So as the friend of the bridegroom, John's compassionate heart and rough words would shake up this people. In other words, he wasn't a meek and mild person. He was intense and desired to be heard because

God had called him! He wasn't just looking for a ticket to heaven, but was pointing to the One that would get us there.

Another illustration of the friends of the bridegroom is found in Matthew 22:2-3:

> *"The kingdom of heaven is like a certain king who arranged a marriage for his son, and sent out his servants to call those who were invited to the wedding."*

We know this as the parable of the wedding feast. I see it as the friends of the bridegroom being sent out by the Father, reminding those who in reality had already been invited. We know that this parable ends badly, but the point I'm trying to make is that the Father already had friends and was sending them out as friends of the bridegroom, inviting the bride to come. We see that it doesn't end well for many given that they didn't see any need to become a bride. Even the guest who was not wearing a wedding garment didn't see a need to prepare for a wedding. It says that he was shocked because he was rejected. He thought he was good enough on his own efforts.

Another illustration is the parable of the faithful and the evil servant recorded in Matthew 24:45-51. What if John the Baptist would have responded as the servant did in verse 48 and 49.

> *"The evil servant said in his heart, 'My master is delaying his coming', and so he begins to beat his fellow servants and to eat and drink with drunkards."*

I think that if I were to see John talking to the crowds as he did, that he might be the evil servant! But we know that God had His hand on this man from the beginning. He might have gotten impatient at times waiting for Jesus to come; but as my favorite saying goes, "God loves the struggle." In it, the friend of the bridegroom must let God work patience or else end up like the evil servant; beating our brothers and sisters. God is calling to those who will love the

Bridegroom yet also love the bride and desire greatly to see her prepare for His return. We are living in days of great turmoil and Jesus desires us to be with Him. If God told Moses that no one could see His face and live, how can we expect to stand before God as the bride of His Son when we are locked up, screwed up, messed up, and having no room for repentance?

I believe what I am about to share with you is the key to us preparing ourselves as the Lamb's bride. I would like to look at the lukewarm church of Laodicea. Jesus said they were neither cold nor hot, but lukewarm and because of this He would spit them out of His mouth. Why were they lukewarm? By observation they were blessed by God with wealth and riches and didn't really have need of anything. Jesus sees something deeper than what comfort and ease will provide. He sees a poor and miserable heart. He sees eyes that have become blind and unperceptive. In fact He sees a heart that has become wretched because of the desire for finding satisfaction in temporary things. The remedy for all of this is fire, purification, and eye salve. Then He makes a statement to the church of Laodicea that has been used by thousands of evangelists over many decades in order to see people saved:

> *"Behold, I stand at the door and knock. If anyone hears My voice and opens the door, I will come in to him and dine with him, and he with Me"* (Revelation 3:20).

You might have seen a painting with Jesus standing at a door knocking, wanting to come into the house. It is a very good painting and the artist was talented, but I don't see this as relating to this verse in Revelation. You might have also seen this verse depicted through video in a restaurant setting with someone sitting at table having dinner with Jesus. I don't believe this is a correct portrayal of this verse either. Look at what Jesus says!

> *"If anyone hears My voice and opens the door, **I will come into him and dine with him.**"* (emphasis mine)

Yes, Jesus is a gentleman, but He is also called the Lion of Judah. Lions devour their prey. Now lest you think that I have gone off my rocker, let me share another verse with you. Jesus makes another statement that even many of His disciples had a hard time with.

> *"Whoever eats My flesh and drinks My blood has eternal life . . . He who eats My flesh and drinks My blood **abides in Me, and I in Him**"* (John 6:54,46 – emphasis mine).

Compare Revelation 3:20,

> ***"I will come in to him and dine with him, and he with Me."*** (emphasis mine)

Dining is the right word to call this, but I prefer the word devouring. It makes more sense because we are so prone to following other lovers, being dumb sheep, and being lead about by our own desires. We need to be devoured; yet we also need to devour Him. I believe this is the marriage supper of the Lamb; devouring and being devoured! If you have trouble with this terminology think of yourself as devouring His word, His character, His brilliance, His untainted emotions, and His holiness. Then see Jesus devouring all your shortcomings, your failings, your wicked intent, your lustful eyes, and your cutting words. Remember it says we are marrying a Lamb and not a person. Very important! The Lamb represents something far more than just a person. Since the days of Abraham, a lamb had a very special significance in regard to Isaac, who was God's promised son to Abraham. Abraham's descendants also saw the Lamb and it's blood on their doorposts as having special significance in their exodus from Egypt. Behold the Lamb of God who takes away the sin of the world was John the Baptist's proclamation when he saw Jesus. The first thing that the apostle John saw in Revelation was Jesus glorified with a face like the sun. He then saw a slain Lamb standing throughout the rest of the book. God portrayed His only Son as a slain Lamb standing! Let us be glad and rejoice, for the **marriage of the Lamb** has come, and His wife has made herself ready! She makes herself ready to marry a

Lamb. (Very important observation!) As you can see below throughout the book of Revelation it's all about the Lamb!

> *I looked, and behold, in the midst of the throne and of the four living creatures, and in the midst of the elders, **stood a Lamb as though it had been slain**.*
>
> ***He (the Lamb)*** *came and took the scroll out of the right hand of Him who sat on the throne.*
>
> *When **He (the Lamb)** had taken the scroll, the four living creatures and the twenty-four elders **fell down before the Lamb**.*
>
> ***You (the Lamb)*** *are worthy to take the scroll, and to open its seals; for **You were slain**, and have redeemed us by **Your blood**.*
>
> *Worthy is the **Lamb** that was slain.*
>
> *Blessing and honor and glory and power be to Him who sits on the throne, and to the **Lamb** forever and ever.*
>
> *Now I saw when the **Lamb** opened one of the seals.*
> *When **He (the Lamb)** opened the second seal.*
> *When **He (the Lamb)** opened the third seal.*
> *When **He (the Lamb)** opened the fourth seal.*
> *When **He (the Lamb)** opened the fifth seal.*
> *When **He (the Lamb)** opened the sixth seal.*
> *When **He (the Lamb)** opened the seventh seal.*
>
> *The kings of the earth, the great men, the rich men, the commanders, the mighty men, every slave and every free man, hid themselves . . . and said hide us from the face of Him who sits on the throne and from the **wrath of the Lamb**.*

*A great multitude which no one could number . . . standing before the throne and before the **Lamb**.*

*They washed their robes and made them white in the **blood of the Lamb**.*

*For the **Lamb** who is in the midst of the throne will shepherd them.*

*All who dwell on the earth will worship him, whose names have not been written in the **Book of the Lamb**.*

*Then I looked, and behold, **a Lamb standing on Mount Zion**, and with **Him** one hundred and forty-four thousand.*

*These are the ones who **follow the Lamb** wherever **He** goes.*

*These were redeemed from among men, being first fruits to God and to the **Lamb**.*

*He shall be tormented with fire and brimstone in the presence of the holy angels and in the **presence of the Lamb**.*

*They sing the song of Moses, the servant of God, and the **song of the Lamb**.*

*These will **make war with the Lamb**, and the **Lamb** will overcome them.*

*The **marriage of the Lamb** has come.*

The marriage supper of the Lamb.

*The wall of the city had twelve foundations, and on them were the names of the **twelve apostles of the Lamb**.*

*I saw no temple in it, for the Lord God Almighty and the **Lamb** are its temple.*

The Lamb is its light.

*He showed me a pure river of water of life, clear as crystal, proceeding from **the throne of God and of the Lamb**.*

*There shall be no more curse, but **the throne of God and of the Lamb** shall be in it.*

Come, I will show you the bride, the Lamb's wife.

(All emphasis in the above Scriptures of Revelation are mine)

THIS IS WHAT THE LAST DAYS OUTPOURING LOOKS LIKE:

"The prophet who has a dream, let him tell a dream; and he who has **My word**, let him **speak My word** faithfully. What is the chaff to the wheat? **Is not My word like a fire**?"
"**His word was in my heart like a burning fire shut up in my bones**!" (Jeremiah 23:28-29, 20:9 – emphasis mine)

The word of the Lord that comes to a person is like a fire. It first consumes within the one that carries it. Then it comes forth with fervent burning and cannot be contained! It hotly consumes all that which is volatile! If we resist His word in disobedience today then we can only expect the fire of His word to consume the chaff in our lives on that Day! My cry is that the Lord would judge me today for any chaff I may have, so that I will enter into His joy on His Day!

THE VOICE OF THE BRIDEGROOM
November 26, 2016

     We just read about John the Baptist in the previous chapter, which mentions him as the friend of the bridegroom. It says in John 3:29, that he rejoiced greatly because he was hearing the bridegroom's voice. Why would John rejoice greatly because of His voice and not the fact that He was now manifested to Israel in the flesh? It would be like me saying to my wife after not seeing her for a few days, "It's really great to hear your voice!" I could only say this if I had just called her on the phone. In seeing her in person, my emphasis would not be on her voice, but on the very fact that she was with me. Her presence would be very much appreciated. Why was the focus of the bridegroom's voice being heard so important? We have to back up a few thousand years in order to set the stage in order to answer this question. This might be hard to read and understand, but please stay with me because it will make sense in the end.

     We read about Israel and how they were in bondage in Egypt. Moses came along and was called by God to become their deliverer.

After ten plagues that only affected Egypt, Israel left that land having plundered the silver and gold from the Egyptians, but ended up wandering the desert for 40 years because of disobedience. Shortly before they were to enter the land of Canaan, God set up a test. We see this test in Deuteronomy 27 and 28.

> *"Keep all the commandments which I command you today . . . set up for yourselves large stones, and white wash them with lime. You shall write very plainly on the stones all the words of this law . . . This day you have become the people of the Lord your God. Therefore you shall obey the voice of the Lord your God, and observe His commandments and His statutes which I command you today . . . These shall stand on Mount Gerizim to bless . . . and these shall stand on Mount Ebal to curse."*
> (Deuteronomy 27:1-13)

This place on these two mountains was a natural amphitheater. Voices could be heard for a long distance. It is from here that we see the blessings and the curses proclaimed to Israel. I will skip over many of these and go directly to verses 54-57 of Deuteronomy 28. Remember the curses were proclaimed upon Israel as a warning if they refused to listen to God's voice and obey Him. Israel was in full agreement with God at this time because after every curse was proclaimed they would answer and say "Amen" (so be it). This is the backdrop for the detailed prophetic words in these next few lines that were proclaimed to Israel in Deuteronomy 28. I believe this curse is foundational to the subject matter of the bridegroom's voice.

> *"The sensitive and very refined man among you will be hostile . . .toward the wife of his bosom . . . so that he will not give any of them the flesh of his children whom he will eat, because he has nothing left in the siege."*

> *"The tender and delicate woman among you . . . will refuse to the husband of her bosom . . . her placenta*

> *. . . and her children whom she bears; for she will eat them secretly for lack of everything in the siege and desperate straits in which your enemy shall distress you at all your gates."*

Moses received these words from the Lord as a warning to Israel. They are prophetic in nature because Israel had not come into the land yet and Jerusalem was not their capital city. Moses proclaimed that this would be one of the results that would happen if they didn't listen to and obey His voice after they entered the land. Many years later after Israel had entered the land of Canaan, she began to ignore God and set up her own ways of worship and living. Prophets began to prophesy to Israel because of her disobedience and concerning the curses in Deuteronomy 27-28; even detailing them. Jeremiah was one of those prophets. In his book, he makes mention of Israel's disobedience and proclaims the result:

> *"Because you have not heard My words, behold, I will send and take all the families of the north says the Lord, and Nebuchadnezzar the king of Babylon, My servant, and I will bring them against this land . . . Moreover **I will take from them** (Israel) . . . **the voice of the bridegroom and the voice of the bride.**"*
> (Jeremiah 25:8-10)

The Lord said He would take the voice of bridegroom and bride away and Israel would serve Babylon 70 years because of disobedience and because of the curses proclaimed on Mt. Ebal. The voice of the bridegroom and the bride represent love speaking. Through Israel's disobedience, she stopped having a relationship with the Lord. She was no longer overjoyed in her relationship with God and sought out other gods that would be more exciting to her flesh. Deuteronomy 28 says that a terrible nation will come against her and horrifying things would happen because of their choices to stray away from their covenant with Him. The siege happened as Babylon surrounded the city blocking all avenues for food going into the city. This in turn created a dire situation leading to starvation, which further led to what was described above: eating their own children who had died in the siege. The voice of the bridegroom and bride are not just heard because their wedding day had come, but also because of their children being born and raised. Jeremiah warned Israel of this many times; as in Jeremiah 7:34, 16:9, and 25:10 that the voice of bridegroom and bride would cease. This was a tragic situation. Many parents lost their children and many children lost their parents. Most of them were carried off as slaves to Babylon. The things that happened were not easily forgotten even after several hundred years. We know that Jerusalem and the Temple were rebuilt after 70 years had gone by, yet the wounds of this tragedy continued to fester. When Jesus came, Israel was occupied by Rome, so their situation wasn't any better. It was at this time that John the Baptist proclaimed Jesus as the Lamb of God who would take away the sin of the world. He also said he rejoiced much because he was hearing the Bridegroom's voice. This wasn't just any bridegroom, this was The Bridegroom of all bridegrooms. Hearing His voice would mean the bride would be emerging from her chambers. Praise God He is coming for a pure and spotless bride! But I'm afraid this isn't the end of this story. There is one more place in Scripture that talks about the silencing of the bride and bridegroom's voice. We find this Scripture in Revelation 18:23.

> *"The voice of the bridegroom and the bride shall not be heard in you anymore."*

This is referring to the harlot woman spoken of in Revelation 17. These two chapters (17 and 18) describe the destruction of the great harlot. I believe by the description of her in verse 4 that she thinks she is a bride because of her attire and adornment.

> *"The woman was arrayed in purple and scarlet, and adorned with gold and precious stones and pearls."*

This had always been bridal attire for engaged or newly wedded couples. Then again in 18:7, she actually says in her heart,

> *"I sit as queen, and am no widow, and will not see sorrow."*

This is her proclamation in the days that Jesus describes as the beginning of sorrows. You will notice in 18:4 that a voice from heaven speaks to believers saying,

> *"Come out of her, my people, lest you share in her sins, and lest you receive of her plagues."*

I take this to mean that there are going to be God's people in and amongst this harlot people. God is about to send judgment on this harlot who has walked away and given herself to other lovers. The woman or harlot mentioned represents a large group of people with a cheep grace ideology. The results that happen in one hour will be that the voice of the bridegroom and the bride will not be heard in her anymore. This is only one of many things that will come upon this harlot. I'm again reminded of the parable of the wheat and tares. The Amplified Version calls the tares "darnel," or weeds that resemble wheat. The true bride is the wheat and the tares are of the harlot. They both grow up together, but God calls the bride to separate from the harlot so that she won't be judged for the same sins as the harlot commits. Notice Revelation 19:2, as the voice of a great multitude speaks from heaven saying,

> *"True and righteous are His judgments, because He has judged the great harlot who corrupted the earth with her fornication."*

The earth and the people on it have been corrupted because of this harlot woman who thinks she is a bride. This is exactly what we see happening today --- people claiming Jesus, but not loving and obeying His voice and living very loosely. The reality of it is that she commits fornication and harlotry against God. So we see the result: the voice of the Bridegroom will not be heard in her anymore! Forever! (Revelation 18:23) I believe with all my heart that Jesus' voice could be heard very plainly in the midst of this harlot, but she turned a deaf ear. His patience in the midst of great evil and wickedness is to be noted. This can also be noticed throughout the prophets toward Israel as well. God was very patient with Israel, yet He continued to proclaim the coming of Babylon for several years before Nebuchadnezzar rode into Jerusalem.

We can rejoice that we have a Bridegroom that is faithful and full of patience. He speaks to us concerning the events that will transpire in the book of Revelation at the very last chapter:

> *"I, Jesus, have sent My angel to testify to you these things in the churches. I am the Root and the Offspring of David, the Bright and Morning Star." And the Spirit and the bride say, "Come!" And let him who hears say, "Come!"*

The Holy Spirit is saying for Jesus to come back! What is the bride saying these days? Is she living in comfort and ease or is her heart longing for His return!!!

THIS IS WHAT THE LAST DAYS OUTPOURING LOOKS LIKE:

"**Suddenly a voice** came out of the cloud, saying, **'This is My beloved Son**, in whom I am well pleased. **Hear Him**!' And when the disciples heard it, **they fell on their faces**!" (Matthew 17:5-6 – emphasis mine)

When all you hear is His voice and all you see is His Son, you can't help but fall on your face!

CALLING DOWN FIRE
November 29, 2016

    Israel had strayed from God and was worshipping Baal. This was during the time of Elijah the prophet. Elijah challenged Ahab to bring four hundred and fifty prophets of Baal to Mount Carmel to offer a sacrifice to the Lord. They were to take a bull and offer it on an altar without fire. Whoever's bull was consumed by fire would be a sign to all that God did it. The Baal prophets killed the bull and even went so far as to jump on the altar and cut themselves in order to invoke Baal to let fire fall on the sacrifice. IT NEVER HAPPENED! Elijah did the very same thing only with a couple differences. He honored God choosing Israel by choosing 12 stones to rebuild the altar. Then he had water poured on the sacrifice three times till it filled the trench around the altar. Elijah prayed and the fire fell from heaven and not only consumed the sacrifice, but also vaporized the water in the trench. The Israelites saw this happen and fell on their faces crying out,

        "The Lord, He is God! The Lord, He is God!" (1Kings 18:39)

This was a powerful sign from God and struck the hearts of all Israel as they observed. It accomplished what it was sent forth to do.

Ahab and Jezebel had a son Ahaziah who became king of Israel after Ahab died. He only reigned two years (1Kings 22:51). In those two short years, Ahaziah injured himself and inquired of Baal to see if he would recover. Elijah again responded to this Baal worship by addressing this king:

> *"Is it because there is no God in Israel that you are going to inquire of Baal?"* (2Kings 1:3)

Ahaziah burned with anger and sent a captain with fifty men to capture Elijah. At the confrontation Elijah proclaimed,

> *"If I am a man of God, let fire come down from heaven and consume you and your fifty men."*

IT HAPPENED! This confrontation happened three times with three different companies of men. The third time, the fear of God fell on them and they cried out for mercy. They were not consumed! The purpose of sharing these two stories is to point out that fire fell in both situations. It was a miraculous sign from God, and caused the fear of the Lord to fall on those involved.

We see this very same thing happen in another place in Scripture, only in a different setting with different results. Revelation 13:11-13 speaks of a beast (a man) that performs miraculous signs in order to deceive people into worshipping a false god empowered by Satan himself. It says that he even makes fire come down from heaven to be seen by men. This man just did what Elijah had done, only as a sign to deceive! What I see happening this very day in and through the election process has me sending a warning to believers. Men are looking for a leader who will establish for them all they desire in order to live happy and carefree. We see this in the USA every time there is an election, and we also see this happen in other countries that have free elections. The problem that I see with this focus is that we are looking to a man for answers and not God. Even Christians are caught up in this frenzy.

They are also looking for a man to lead, only with righteous standards (if that is at all possible). Ultimately every one seems to be looking for a man to bring them what they need to live happy. We know that fulfillment in life only comes from God, but many believe that God raises up leaders to bring this as well. This is a very dangerous paradigm to live in! No President or leader will lead us into the kingdom of God. Matthew 24:23-24 addresses this with a warning to us who believe:

> *"If anyone says to you, 'Look, here is the Christ!' do not believe it. For false christs and false prophets will rise and show great signs and wonders to deceive, if possible, even the elect."*

I am not referring to a president, but a Great Deceiver! This pursuit of a man to lead is a prelude to what is to come. Every election produces more turmoil about who becomes the leader. When the leader fails our expectations, we then look for another leader who will fulfill those expectations. This is the ultimate set up for the anti-christ to perform miraculous signs to deceive the very elect! Look what happened to the people in Elijah's day when they saw the fire of God fall from the sky; they fell on their faces! This will be the response to the anti-christ as he performs his incredible signs and wonders for all to see. They will be awestruck by this man! We must not even begin to think that we will recognize this man and immediately reject him. If you are not grounded in Scripture (I'm speaking of the living words of God in the Bible and not just words on a page), then you will most likely fall for this man. I see this time in history to be very troublesome and people in the world will be very desperate. At present, we are on the edge of this happening as we speak! Desperation is mounting in this world as never before. Violence and upheaval seem to spring up like a quick fused rocket spreading its destruction everywhere. Because of social media, the spread of lies and misinformation spews out at the push of a button. Growing in our knowledge of Jesus Christ will be vitally important; otherwise, we will fall for this man thinking he has the power of God in his life! Jesus said that when this occurred, it would be a time of very great tribulation, so His warning should be taken very seriously. He also said that His return would be as in the days of Noah: they were eating and drinking and pursuing sexual relations; completely ignoring the prophet Noah as he built the Ark for a period of 120 years. Then the rain came! If we ignore His warnings, what hope do we have of eternal life? The Lord warns us through His own people, like Noah in his day. I see people ignoring the signs that Jesus told us to look for. Because of this very thing, we are living as in the days of Noah! We can't eat, drink, play, build, plant, marry and ignore the words of Jesus: *"Whosoever desires to save his life will lose it, but whoever loses his life for My sake will find it."* (Matthew 16:25) If we love our life here, and we ignore the words of Jesus, our choice just might be to embrace and follow the man of sin; the great deceiver---the one who promises peace on earth under his rule and authority. You can react to this statement, but this truth in Jesus' words is played out in lives day after day. Picking up your cross means you are walking toward your death! This is following Jesus!

THIS IS WHAT THE LAST DAYS OUTPOURING LOOKS LIKE:

"Then **the Lord opened Balaam's eyes**, and there was the Angel of the Lord standing in the way with His drawn sword in His hand; and **he bowed his head and fell flat on his face**." (Numbers 22:31 – emphasis mine)

The fear of the Lord will fall on His enemies and even cause them to fall on their face! We must pray that the Lord will consume every ounce of greed within our lives because the love of money is the root of all evil. Balaam loved money and his prophetic voice was tainted by greed. His end was soon to come because he thought he could hide from God what was in his heart. Even the donkey had more perception than Balaam. Greed is a very subtle thing. It comes in many faces and expresses itself through many voices. Greed was manifested in Ananias and Sapphira's life. They conspired to deceive people, but mistakenly endeavored to deceive God also. They fell down never to rise again. (Acts 5) I believe that even the wicked will fall on their faces before God in this last days outpouring!

LOVE NEVER FAILS

November 30, 2016

1Corinthians 13:
"Though I (Paul) *speak with the tongues of men and angels . . .*
"Though I (Paul) *have the gift of prophecy . . .*
"Though I (Paul) *understand all mysteries and all knowledge . . .*
"Though I (Paul) *have all faith, so that I could remove mountains . . .*
"Though I (Paul) *bestow all my goods to feed the poor . . .*
"Though I (Paul) *give my body to be burned . . .*
. . . but have not love, I (Paul) *am nothing!"*

What is love and what does it look like? Was Paul walking in love?

The same person who wrote 1 Corinthians 13 also wrote 1 Corinthians 3:9-17 (emphasis mine)

> *"You are God's building . . . let each one take heed how he builds on it. No other foundation can anyone lay than that which is laid, which is Jesus*

> *Christ. Each one's work will become clear; for the Day will declare it . . . by fire . . . and will test each one's work. If anyone's work is burned, he will suffer loss; but he himself will be saved, yet so as through fire. Do you not know that you are the temple of God . . .* ***If anyone defiles the temple of God, God will destroy him. For the temple of God is holy, which temple you are.***" (emphasis mine)

These are strong words for one who claims that he walks in love. Paul learned to walk in love, yet his vision was not clouded by a nebulous love. He had seen the fiery passion of the Lord for holiness to be established in His own people so Paul endeavored to walk in the Father's heart. We are to have that same heart that God the Father has!

The same person who wrote 1 Corinthians 13 also wrote 1 Corinthians 5 (emphasis mine).

> *"It is actually reported that there is sexual immorality among you, and such sexual immorality as is not even named among the Gentiles---that a man has his father's wife! And you are puffed up . . .* ***For I indeed****, as absent in body but present in spirit,* ***have already judged him who has done this deed****. In the name of our Lord Jesus Christ, when you are gathered together, along with my spirit, with the power of our Lord Jesus Christ,* ***deliver such a one to Satan for the destruction of the flesh, that his spirit may be saved.***"

To many Christians, this is a very harsh word and is not love! But Paul continues in 1 Corinthians 5:9:

> *"I wrote to you in my epistle not to keep company with sexually immoral people. Yet I certainly did not mean with the sexually immoral people of this world, or with covetous, or extortioners, or idolaters, since then you would need to go out of the*

> *world.* ***But now I have written to you not to keep company with anyone named a brother****, who is sexually immoral* (shacking up, in support of gay marriage, porn, etc), *or covetous* (longing for what your neighbor has---wife, money, house, car, position, popularity), *idolater* (lover of money and things), *or a reviler* (a person with a foul tongue [railing, abusing, reviling, slandering]---AMP), *or a drunkard* (wine sipping for a buzz, living in Margarita Ville, attending Brew and Bible studies), *or an extortioner* (swindler, charging high interest rates), *not even to eat with such a person. . .* ***Therefore put away from yourselves the evil person.***" (emphasis mine)

I ask you, is this love? YES!!! The very reason the Church is so anemic and powerless today is because we are so afraid of offending someone who proclaims to be a believer yet continues to **willfully** walk in sin. Paul was not afraid of gently confronting those who claimed to be Christians, but had rotten fruit. He knew God was holy! In 1 Corinthians 3, Paul addresses those who build with wood, hay, and stubble and says their works will be burned up. What is important to point out is that Paul then says that if anyone defiles the temple, God will destroy him. I'm not sure what Paul means when he says this, but it doesn't sound good. If God's temple is made of pure transparent gold and we build on it with wood, are we not defiling the integrity of the temple? How do we build on it with wood? By following the same examples that Paul brings out in 1 Corinthians 5 -- sexual immorality (porn, desiring sexually another person), covetousness (greed, love of money), reviler (one who can't control his tongue). This is why Paul said to have nothing to do with them because their willfulness to sin will cling to those who associate with them. This is the very man who wrote chapter 13 "The Love Chapter". God is love and:

> *All Scripture is given by inspiration of God, and is profitable for doctrine, for reproof, for correction, for instruction in righteousness, that the man of God*

> *may be thoroughly equipped for every good work"* (2 Timothy 3:16-17).

If there is no correction, reproof or instruction (Fire!) that causes gold and silver to come forth purified; then wood, hay, and stubble will be the building materials of this generation. All that we have done will be tested with fire. I believe the harlot of the last days will have only built with these materials because of what Revelation 18:8 says,

> *"Her plagues will come in one day---death and mourning and famine. And she will be **utterly burned with fire**, for strong is the Lord God who judges her."*

We must heed the words spoken by the Lord just before this was proclaimed. He exhorts us, His people, to come out of her lest we share in her sins and receive her plagues. I ask the Lord for my own life---judge me now, so I won't come under judgment later on in that day! Lest you think we won't be judged, please, please, please, revisit 1 Corinthians 3-5.

THIS IS WHAT THE LAST DAYS OUTPOURING LOOKS LIKE?

"And one of the ten, **when he saw that he was healed**, returned, and with a loud voice glorified God, and **fell down on his face at His feet**, giving Him thanks!" (Luke 17:15-16 – emphasis mine)

One came out from the camp of the selfish hearted and fell on his face, was rescued, and then filled with praise and adoration for God's goodness! Weren't there nine others who were healed? Are we thankful for what God has done in our lives no matter how small it is, or do we walk away with the mentality that we deserve what we receive because we boast that we are children of the King? Ungratefulness is a wicked, wicked state-of-mind!

SINCERE, BUT IGNORANT
December 3, 2016

    Recently I listened to a video of a couple that were sharing about what God had said to them concerning what the seven thunders of Revelation 10:3-4 had spoken. The man had written down all the words that God had spoken to Him and proceeded to read these words. The words were in great detail and spoken by the man with confidence and authority. I listened; but as I listened, I couldn't help but feel the fear of the Lord well up inside me. This was my response after listening to these words:

    God had told John to seal up what the seven thunders had spoken. In other words, he wasn't to write them down. And if he wasn't to write them, then he wasn't to speak them out to anyone. That would have been disobedience to what God had said. I was reminded of another situation that was very similar to this. In 2 Corinthians 12:4, Paul was caught up to heaven and heard inexpressible words, which was not lawful for a man to utter. God had sealed these words from being spoken by Paul as He also had done with John.

So my question is this: If God told Paul and John not to utter the words that they heard, why do we think God will tell them to us? If we had been alive in Paul's day and were to ask him what he had heard while in paradise, what do you think he would have said to us? If we were to have the opportunity to ask John what the seven thunders said, what would be his response? How can we approach God so arrogantly on these things thinking He will show us, when he told Paul and John not even to speak them? I would say that Paul is the only one who knows what he heard in paradise! John having heard the seven thunders speak from heaven is the **only one** who knows what they said! God established this and He isn't a man that He should lie (or even exaggerate)! He means what He says! On the other hand, God revealed to Daniel tremendous things regarding the last days. Daniel didn't have a clue as to what the interpretation was for the things that he saw. He kept asking for understanding, but God answered him at the end of his book in Daniel 12:4,

> *"But you, Daniel, shut up the words, and seal the book until the time of the end."*

The only difference between what John had heard spoken by the thunders and what Daniel had heard spoken by angels was the word "until"! Until means there is a certain time or season that it will be disclosed and understood. JOHN DID NOT HEAR THE WORD "UNTIL".

What are we to make of these things? It is as in Matthew 24:5,

> *"Many will come in My name, saying, 'I am the Christ,' and will deceive many."*

Christ means anointed one to speak. Notice they come in Jesus' name! We must also notice what He says in verses 11-12,

> *"Then many false prophets will rise up and deceive many. And because lawlessness will abound, the love of many will grow cold."*

I believe these people that spoke of the seven thunders were sincere in what they thought they heard. The key to being a true prophet or a false prophet is obedience; the exact opposite of lawlessness. Lawless people can be sincere in their own deception. This is why we must know the word and know God's heart in His word. If He says seal it up, He means seal it up! If it's sealed up, then who on God's earth can ever hear what was said this side of eternity? He will not violate His own words. Here's the truth: If a prophet speaks today, and his words are not grounded in Biblical truth and obedience to Biblical truth then he is a "sincere (?)," but "false" prophet.

THIS IS WHAT THE LAST DAYS OUTPOURING LOOKS LIKE:

"When the people of Ashdod arose early in the morning, **there was Dagon, fallen on its face** to the earth **before the ark** (the presence) **of the Lord.**"
(1Samuel 5:3 – emphasis mine)

Demons will bow and fall on their faces in the very presence of the Lord! Demons believe in Jesus, yet tremble with fear. We believe and are sometimes very brazen in our lifestyles before the Lord! How can this be? Even demons see and perceive much clearer than many of God's people. Relationship with God is not a right; it's a gift. In the days ahead we will see many demons bow before the Name of Jesus! Ultimately we will see the ruler of all demons bow as he is thrown into the lake of fire!

PERDITION
December 6, 2016

What in the world does this word even mean?

Many today believe that Antiochus IV Epiphanes was the antichrist (the man of sin, or son of perdition) that Paul speaks of in 2 Thessalonians. They believe this because he attacked the second temple and defiled it by sacrificing a pig on the altar and erecting a statue of Zeus, representing himself, in the temple.[2] This display of rancor was very obvious that he was just a wicked ruler and not the antichrist. First of all to offer a pig is a tremendous abomination to Jews and would have been very repelling to them. He wasn't trying to deceive them; he was endeavoring to strongly offend them. The man of sin or antichrist will be far more suave and charismatic in order to win the masses. In the next few paragraphs, I will endeavor to define the word "perdition" which has been used in Scripture a few times but has been deleted from Christian vocabulary.

---

[2] https://en.wikipedia.org/wiki/Son_of_perdition

Whenever I would read through the Bible and see this word, I would just pass over it because of it's undefined obscurity, even though I knew it had eternal consequences attached to it. I had been doing this for 40+ years. Pretty sad, huh! Today, the Lord opened my understanding on the meaning of this word in Scripture.

To begin, we will look at some Scriptures in which this word is found:

> *"Those who desire to be rich **fall into temptation and a snare**, and into many foolish and harmful lusts which drown men in destruction and **perdition.**"* (1Timothy 6:9 – emphasis mine)

> *"For yet a little while, and He who is coming will come and will not tarry. Now the just shall live by faith; but **if anyone draws back**, My soul has no pleasure in him. But we are not of those **who draw back to perdition**, but of those who believe to the saving of the soul."*
> (Hebrews 10:37-39 – emphasis mine)

> *"The heavens and the earth . . . are reserved for fire until the day of judgment and **perdition of ungodly men.**"* (2Peter 3:7 – emphasis mine)

As we see, in these verses, the people mentioned either fell into or drew back into perdition. In looking at the definition of perdition, all sources researched would show the words "to lose" in their definition. If someone where to lose something it would stand to reason that they either had it at one point or it was within their grasp, but they let it slip away. Thus, they either fell away from it or drew back away from what was presented to them. We see a perfect example of this portrayed within Scripture. It's a story that's almost too hard to present, because it touches our very soul and causes us to search our own hearts lest we fall into the same loss. This man walked with Jesus for 3 years. He had seen miracles, healings, and the dead raised. He had also heard words spoken that no other man on earth had ever heard before. John who was the writer of

1 John 1:1 expounds on the beauty of his experience with Jesus:

> *"That which was from the beginning, which **we** have heard, which **we** have seen with our eyes, which **we** have looked upon, and **our** hands have handled, concerning the Word of life."* (emphasis mine)

When John uses the word "we," he was including Judas Iscariot. Judas had seen that which was from the beginning! He had heard and seen Jesus with his own eyes! He had looked upon, handled, and even embraced Jesus! John, who was also the writer of the Gospel of John, recorded the words of Jesus spoken concerning Judas:

> *"While I was with them, I kept and preserved them in Your Name [in the knowledge and worship of You]. Those You have given Me I guarded and protected, and not one of them has perished or is lost **except the son of perdition [Judas Iscariot**--the one who is now doomed to destruction, destined to be lost], that the Scripture might be fulfilled."* (John 17:12 — AMP – emphasis mine)

It's a daunting thing that the Scripture had to be fulfilled; yet Judas chose to walk into this destiny of destruction. Those of us who believe are destined for eternal life, yet as we have seen in the Scriptures, some draw back because of various sins and some fall into a snare because of the desire to be rich. Within these examples, we see that they had once believed but had fallen; losing that which they had. Judas fell and lost what he had also. These mentioned were closely associated with Jesus through faith at one point in time, but removed themselves from faith and pulled back to perdition. Jesus has never called, never will call, one of His followers a son of perdition; no matter how much they have struggled, slipped, tripped, stumbled, and fallen. If we are enamored by the desire to have wealth or refuse to repent of a certain sin in our life, we could face perdition (the loss of eternal life) as is the definition of perdition in the NKJV Thompson Chain Reference Bible. The point I would like to make is that we have been presented with eternal life in the Son of

God. If we choose a road that leads away from holiness and intimacy with Jesus, then all could be lost forever!

TWO SONS OF PERDITION

What I have said up to this point will make a whole lot more sense after what I share in the next few paragraphs. As God's people we have a deep desire to see Jesus return and be with Him forever. I believe that day is approaching fast and we could very well see it in our lifetime. Paul addresses a significant event that happens before Jesus comes. He describes this event in 2 Thessalonians 2:1-3:

> *"Now, brethren, concerning the coming of our Lord Jesus Christ and our gathering together to Him, we ask you, not to be soon shaken in mind or troubled, either by spirit or by word or by letter, as if from us, as though the day of Christ had come. Let no one deceive you by any means;* **for that Day will not come unless the falling away comes first, and the man of sin is revealed, the son of perdition."**
> (emphasis mine)

Didn't Jesus just call Judas the son of perdition? What do these two have in common? Could it be that both had something very precious within their grasp, yet chose to walk a different road? The only difference between Judas and the man of sin is that the man of sin will bring about the great falling away. Many will see him as their Messiah and will be lead away to destruction. Because of great signs and wonders he will deceive, if possible, even the elect. As it says, the man of sin is revealed in conjunction with the falling away because of his lying signs and wonders. 2Thessalonians 2:9 goes on to say:

> *"The coming of the lawless one is according to the working of Satan, with all power, signs, and lying wonders, and with all unrighteous deception among those who perish, because* **they did not receive the love of the truth,** *that they might be saved."* (emphasis mine)

This is exactly what happened to Judas Iscariot! He did not receive the love of the truth! Judas was sent out by Jesus just as all the other disciples had been. He had seen miracles and healings and deliverance through his own life just as all the others. Judas was guilty of what Jesus describes in Matthew 7:22-23-concerning those who had done miracles in His name:

> *"Depart from Me, you who practice lawlessness!"*

Matthew 24:12 also mentions this lawlessness:

> *"And because lawlessness will abound, the love of many will grow cold."*

This describes the falling away to the man of lawlessness. Their love for the Lord Jesus grew cold possibly because of His delay in coming back and also being offended at all the wickedness that seemingly looked to be ignored by Him. This man will take these people by storm! This man is also described in Revelation 17:7,

> *"The beast that you saw was, and is not, and will ascend out of the bottomless pit **and go to perdition.**"* (emphasis mine)

This beast is one and the same as the man of sin or the son of perdition. It describes him in Revelation 13:11 as having two horns like a lamb yet speaking like a dragon with tremendous deception. The fact that he was, and is not, and will ascend from the bottomless pit and go to perdition is an exact contrast or opposite of that which is proclaimed of Jesus:

> *"He who was and is and is to come, the Almighty."*
> (Revelation 1:8)

If perdition means to lose, then this man of sin may have had some kind of encounter with the Lord, yet turned violently away and lost everything just as Judas did. He will then give himself completely to Satan and his will. This man of sin could go undetected in the midst of believers just as Judas did in the midst of the Apostles. In John's letter he writes about the antichrist coming, but also that antichrists have already come, and with this he makes a startling comment:

> **"They went out from us**, but they were not of us; for if they had been of us, they would have continued with us; but they went out that they might be made manifest, that none of them were of us." (1John 2:19 – emphasis mine)

This is exactly how it was with Judas! Jesus was the only one who knew Judas' heart; all the others didn't have a clue! This is a cause for complete and unhindered surrender to the lordship of Jesus and the Holy Spirit. He knows our weakness, and as Steve Camp sang so beautifully in one of his songs: "But for now He covers me!" We must have His covering upon us as Noah had his covering in the Ark!

In conjunction with the falling away we have to look at Revelation 17 again. Verse 3 describes a woman sitting on a scarlet beast that has the same description of the beast in Revelation 13---seven heads and ten horns with names of blasphemy. The woman that John was observing was described as a bride because of her adornment; yet she has on her forehead the words Mother of harlots. I believe Revelation chapters 17 and 18 describe the great falling away vicariously through this woman. She once knew the Lord as Judas did, but she did not receive the love of the truth. She gave up on Jesus Christ and turned to the man of sin who did tremendous miracles and won her heart! Notice chapter 18:2:

> "Babylon the great (the woman) *is fallen, is fallen, and has become a dwelling place of demons, a prison for every foul spirit, and cage for every unclean and hated bird!"*

She has fallen away, believed on, and followed the son of perdition! It just stated the words "she has become", which would mean she was something else before she became a dwelling of demons. This woman represents a large group of people. I believe they followed Jesus at one time from a distance, but then became like the ones described in 1 Timothy 6:9---pursuing riches, the love of money, and worldly possessions. I believe this because of what Revelation 18 starting at verse 9 says.

> *"All the kings, merchants and those who trade on the sea were weeping, wailing, lamenting and crying out when they saw her destruction because she is not buying their merchandise anymore!"*

She was not buying their merchandise because she was destroyed! She had been caught up in luxury items and riches! It says her destruction happens in one hour! Again, as I have said before, it's no wonder there is a loud cry in Revelation 18:4 that says:

> **"Come out of her, my people, lest you share in her sins, and lest you receive of her plagues."** (emphasis mine)

THIS IS WHAT THE LAST DAYS OUTPOURING LOOKS LIKE:

"So he **(Gabriel) came near** where I (Daniel) stood, and when he came **I was afraid and fell on my face**; but **he said to me, 'Understand**, son of man.' "
(Daniel 8:17 – emphasis mine)

To understand the times and seasons that are upon us is of utmost importance. If we are dull and lack spiritual understanding, then we will fall on our face before anything resembling miraculous angelic presence! This is what the man of sin will look like in the last days when he comes. Will he be recognized for what he is or will the delaying of Jesus' coming cause dullness of heart and a desperation that will cause Christians to fall for any miraculous angelic presence that comes? He who endures to the end will be saved!

WHAT WAS GOD THINKING?
December 9, 2016

"For I know the thoughts that I think toward you, says the Lord, thoughts of peace and not of evil, to give you a future and a hope. Then you will call upon Me and go and pray to Me, and I will listen to you. And you will seek Me and find Me, when you search for Me with all your heart." (Jeremiah 29:11-13)

    These words have been heard in dozens, if not hundreds, of sermons throughout the past 30-40 years. I have received much comfort from these words when I found myself in trouble spiritually or just spending a stint in the wilderness. I'm sure you have quoted these words over your own life or even others who seem to be having a real tough time in life. These words speak the very heart of God to us and we receive His love and comfort through them. We love it when God affirms us and it propels us towards seeking His face. Even though we love these words from God, they are usually taken out of context. I will endeavor to explain in the next two examples below.

    The first example will be Jeremiah 29:11-13; put in the context of the rest of the story that surrounds these words in chapter

29. The second example will be the same, only from what has been my perspective; because of all the sermons I had heard over the years on this subject and never having studied it myself. I will quote the verses in italics, but add the reality of both perspectives in my own words.

GOD'S PERPSECTIVE

Scripture	God's Perspective
"For I know the thoughts that I think toward you, says the Lord . . ."	My thoughts are to send you into Babylon because you have consistently disobeyed My voice and have pursued other things. I warned you of this through Moses in Deuteronomy 28:47-57 when I spoke of a nation of fierce countenance coming against you because you refused to obey My voice. Through this hardship I will tenderize your heart and once again capture your attention so that I will be first place in your life.
". . . thoughts of peace and not of evil . . ."	I spoke to you, and My thoughts were for you to seek the peace of Babylon, the evil nation that carried you away to your new home. That you should pray for peace to be upon Babylon so that you also could live in peace. Because in Babylon's peace you will have peace. (Jeremiah 29:7)
". . . to give you a future and a hope."	You will find this hope as you live in Babylon and endure the hardship that I have sent you into. As you take wives and have children in Babylon you will increase and not decrease. This is your future when I bring you back from Babylon. I have not determined evil against you, but have disciplined you as a son. No son is without discipline otherwise you are a illegitimate son. (Jeremiah 29:6)

"Then you will call upon Me and go and pray to Me, and I will listen to you."	When you find yourselves living in Babylon, then you will pray and call on My name because you will find yourselves in a foreign land next door to neighbors who live and do things that you are not accustomed to. You will be a stranger in a very strange land with people observing you with scrutiny and criticism, yet it will cause you to cry out to Me and seek Me with all of your heart! Don't be discouraged! I will listen to you! (Jeremiah 29:11-15)
"And you will seek Me and find Me, when you search for Me with all your heart."	Don't be like your brethren who disobeyed Me and didn't go to Babylon with you. They stayed in Jerusalem because they thought I would deliver them from Babylon, yet I sent the sword, famine, pestilence, and a curse upon them because they did not heed My words. You are different because you heeded My words and set your heart to seek Me. As you seek Me with all your heart you will find Me as you live in Babylon! (Jeremiah 29:16-20)

MY PERSPECTIVE

"For I know the thoughts that I think toward you, says the Lord . . ."	This is how I always heard it preached: God has big plans for me. I will be used by God to perform miracles and healings and bring glory to His name. Yes, God has big plans! They might start out small, but be faithful and He will make them big. Can you relate to this?

". . . thoughts of peace and not of evil . . ."	Again, this is how I heard it preached: *"Plans to prosper you and not to harm you."* God will cause me to prosper no matter what I put my hand to. He is all about prospering His children. No child of God should be down or depressed, sad or bummed out (old hippy term). God is not out to harm us and He is always for us so we won't have to be bummed out! God is going to give me the wealth of the nations, so get ready! God is always on my side and anything He does will make me walk with a smile and be joyful! If anything bad comes upon me it's the Devil and he must be rebuked from my life; otherwise, the bad thing that came upon me is because of my own sin. NOTE: The translation I always heard preached used the word "prosper" instead of "peace". Since they were to seek the peace of Babylon, using the word prosperity would mean something altogether different. God was not concerned about prospering Babylon, but He was concerned that they would have peace, because He had sent His people their to be re-adjusted in their lives and thinking. Peace in Babylon was very significant at that point in time because it meant peace for His people.
". . . to give you a future and a hope."	If God's thoughts towards me are for peace and to give me a future, then I should go out and celebrate this fact. So why not buy a bag of donuts or snickers bars and celebrate! After all, how can it get any better than to have peace and a future! The hope that I was seeing had to do with my success as a Christian. Everyone I would meet or share the gospel with should be instantly saved and miraculously changed so I could be affirmed as a dynamic and fruitful believer. If this didn't happen my future looked very bleak!

"Then you will call upon Me and go and pray to Me, and I will listen to you."	Simply put: If God has plans to prosper me and I believe it, then when I pray in faith He will always hear me and answer my prayers. Saints, it doesn't get any better than this! Jesus said whatever I ask in His name He will give it. If my prayers are not being answered, then there is something wrong in my life! Beloved, this was not what Israel was thinking at the time!
"And you will seek Me and find Me, when you search for Me with all your heart."	If God's thoughts are for me to prosper because of His great plans for me; then if I seek Him, I will always find Him. It was never told me that God sometimes hides Himself! So once again I'm introspecting because I think I've ticked Him off somehow and He is ignoring me. "Hey God! You have big plans for me! Why are You not showing up so I can see them come to pass?" I've learned since then that "God loves the struggle!" He hides so we will search through thorns and thickets (if we have to) in order to find Him. This deepens our relationship with Him when it's a struggle to find Him.

    I'm sure everyone that has heard these verses preached has a different interpretation of what they mean. The main thing that I wanted to point out was that they are usually taken out of context and used for personal uplifting. If we were to talk with an Israelite from that era, they would interpret it much differently then we do. It was very personal to them because everything about their life changed instantly. Their house was gone! Their income was gone! Their livestock was gone! Their freedom was gone! Their way of life in Israel was gone! God wanted their attention! He wanted them to be hearing and obeying. Jesus' words to us today are no different!

    "He who loves Me, obeys My commandments!"

WHAT DOES THE LAST DAYS OUTPOURING LOOK LIKE?

"**You will not need to fight in this battle**. Position yourselves, **stand still and see** the salvation of the Lord. And Jehoshaphat bowed his head **with his face to the ground**, and all Judah and **the inhabitants of Jerusalem bowed** before the Lord, **worshiping** the Lord." (2Chronicles 20:17-18 – emphasis mine)

True worship causes us to stand still and just let God engage the enemy as we again fall on our face before Him! How can we (myself included) be so arrogant as to think the defeat of evil and demons in our lives is only because we have been given the authority to do so? If this be the case, Jesus would have never suffered and been crucified because He had been given ultimate authority! He could have sidestepped the cross, but He didn't! He bowed and stood still, as a lamb to the slaughter, and let God bring about His resurrection. Our shouting, yelling, and screaming at the devil will only work if we have seen who we are in Christ and what He has established in us through His death and resurrection. It's not us taking authority! It's us standing in His! Sampson had the anointing, yet walked in a very fleshly lifestyle. Who are we to think we can do the same and work the works of God? It's arrogance to think we are something special to God and that He will use us in spite of our lawless actions that have nothing to do with His kingdom. God works in and through us because we have yielded ourselves to His holiness. Worship is a lifestyle not a position we find ourselves in on Sunday morning! The twenty-four elders of Revelation sit encircled around the One on the throne and gaze at His beauty, falling on their faces every time His name is mentioned. Have we been so caught up in the world and its delicacies that we can only handle giving Him one or two hours on Sunday and maybe fifteen minutes every other day of the week? Is this what it means to be a disciple? If this be the case, then Peter and the apostles where martyred in vain because they gave Him all of their time! Their lives were wasted if all that pleases Jesus is two hours on Sunday and a few minutes during the week!

WHAT DOES THE LAST DAYS OUTPOURING LOOK LIKE?

     We have all been given a gift! This gift is usually never opened. If it is opened, it's only for a brief moment in order to observe the contents. The contents then are ignored and put aside for a more convenient time. When this convenient time comes it's briefly looked at and then set aside once again. The giver of this gift is heart broken because the gift was given with much love and affection. The heart of the giver is grieved beyond description and we have no idea what that looks like! There are some who open this gift and observe it very ravenously being careful to take in every detail of this gift. This brings the giver great joy because the giver sees the gift as a tremendous catalyst for transformation in the receiver of the gift. This same gift has been given to many people throughout the ages of history since the beginning. Those who have received this gift with sincerity and joy have become predominantly influential people in this earth. The promise within this gift still remains today! Many are seeing this promise and taking its contents very seriously. I see this gift as having taken on flesh and blood.

The Word became flesh and dwelt among us! The Word existed from the beginning and has prevailed throughout time; even prevailing through the slaughter of the innocents and through the darkest times of history that have come upon this earth.

Today the Word still prevails even in the midst of trillions of words spoken. Words, words, words---words of hatred, lust, greed, selfishness, dictatorship. Words from radio, TV, video games, advertisements. Words on FB---words that destroy character, words that kill, words of destruction towards classmates. Pleasant words that are spoken in voice only, but what is in the heart is contrary. I'm reminded of Matthew 24:12 which says,

> *"Because lawlessness will abound, the love of many will grow cold."*

The love for the Word of God (the Bible) will grow cold! The love for the Word made flesh will grow cold! The love for the Word in God's people will grow cold!

I see many seeking to establish new words of God through prophecy, dreams, and visions. Yes, this is what is promised through the Holy Spirit, yet the Scripture seems to take second place in many of these words. God gave us a gift in His Word (the Bible) yet we only glance at it every so often. Even the prophets immersed themselves in the written Word that Moses recorded. The Words of the prophets were always, always, always founded in and through the Scriptures; Scriptures like Deuteronomy 27 and 28. They received the Word and built upon the foundation of the Word that had already been laid since the beginning! Their dreams and visions were founded through the Holy Spirit and God's already established Word. Today we have hundreds of named prophets who have a word. They speak it very authoritatively as if it has come from the very Throne of God! If this be true, why do so many words conflict with each other? IS THE ONE WHO SITS ON THE THRONE CONFUSED? Why do so many words contradict the Bible? We must ask ourselves why this is happening. Is it what Mark 13:6 says?

> *"Many will come in My name, saying, I am He (anointed one), and will deceive many."*

Or is it Matthew 24:11,

> *"Then many false prophets will rise up and deceive many."*

Why is it that I see dozens or even hundreds of prophets on FB and YOUTUBE? Every one of them is running with a certain word! In these days of so many prophetic words we, as followers of Jesus, must be grounded in The Word that has already been established from the beginning. If we are not grounded, then we will listen to any word that comes along that is empowered with signs and wonders. We are living in the last days! Satan knows that his time is growing shorter every year! The heat has been turned up and the words we hear have become louder! We are warned throughout the Bible to examine what is in our hearts because the heart is very deceptive and who can know it? Please take heed and listen to Paul's warning in 1 Corinthians 10:6-12. (emphasis mine)

> *"Now **these things became our examples**, to the intent that we should not lust after evil things as they also lusted. Do not become **idolaters**, as were some of them. As it is written, 'the people sat down to eat and drink, and rose up to play.' Nor let us commit **sexual immorality**, as some of them did, and in one day twenty-three thousand fell; nor let us **tempt Christ**, as some of them also tempted, and were destroyed by serpents; nor **complain**, as some of them also complained, and were destroyed by the destroyer. Now all these things happened to them **as examples**, and they were written **for our admonition**, upon whom the ends of the ages have come. Therefore let him who thinks he stands take heed lest he fall."*

I see today people given to comfort and pleasure as they eat and drink and play. You might only see the people of the world doing these things, but we must take a hard look at those who would call themselves a follower of Jesus. Many of these walk the very same way. You might respond by saying God gives us all things to enjoy, yet consider in the verses above what Paul says. He uses the word "idolatry" in the same sentence as eating, drinking, and playing; we must take this to heart!

Sexual immorality takes on many faces these days. I will not go into detail lest I cause someone to sin, but pornography has become a ravenous animal through the Internet. When I was a teenager, I had to search for pornography. Today, in the age of technology, it searches out and even stalks its victims! This is a major issue, not just with the world, but also with those who follow Jesus! Pastors, evangelists, teachers, prophets; every Church member is affected somehow. Paul warns us in 1 Corinthians 10:8 to consider that 23,000 people fell because of sex in that day (referring to Numbers 25:1-18). Could I be so bold as to say that in this day we live in if this judgment on sex sins were to happen, the number that would fall would be in the millions!

Thinking we know better than God how to run our life is tempting Christ. Jesus told us anyone who would follow Him must also pick up his cross and walk toward his own death. We run from death because we think He has given us all things that pertain to life and godliness. We also proclaim over our life what Jesus said,

> *"I have come that they may have life, and that they may have it more abundantly."* (John 10:10)

This is truth, but if this is only talking about life on earth, then why did He tell His disciples to die the same way as He died? I don't see too many followers of Jesus walking the same way as Jesus walked. We complain when things get too hard! We cry, sigh, and moan if we don't get our way! This is another issue Paul addressed: the destroyer destroyed those that complained. Are we any different from Israel that the destroyer won't come upon us? Does God treat us different than He did with those who complained back in that day? Maybe the fact that God seems to be so quiet these days gives us license to not only complain, but to eat and drink and play and lust and tempt God and live our lives as though He doesn't exist. I call these types of people "Christian atheists." They believe in God, yet they live as though He didn't exist! I must end with a short prayer that I heard a pastor say many, many times several years ago. "Jesus help us!"

THE LAST TRUMPET [EVER]!

January 1, 2017

*"**THEREFORE**, my beloved brethren, be steadfast, immovable, always abounding in the work of the Lord, **knowing** that your labor is **not in vain** in the Lord (**even if you die**)."* (1 Corinthians 15:58 – emphasis mine)

You're probably wondering what this verse has to do with the last trumpet. Please follow with me. I have always looked at this verse as an encouragement to continue to do good things, to be steadfast, and not be discouraged; because in the end, we will be rewarded. Yes, it speaks of not being discouraged, but why? As Bob Mumford has spoken many times in his messages, if there is a "therefore," we must see what it is there for! In looking at this verse in the 15th chapter of 1 Corinthians, let's back up a few verses and see the context of this. In verses 16-17 it gives a snapshot of the context:

> *"If the dead do not rise, then Christ is not risen. And if Christ is not risen, your faith is futile; you are still in your sins!*

If this be true, then our labor would be in vain and we would be lost! The context is obviously addressing the people who have died in Christ, but also those in Jesus who will be dying in the future. If there is no resurrection, then we are all doomed! Look at what verses 18-19 says:

> *"Then also those who have fallen asleep in Christ have perished. **If in this life only** we have hope in Christ, we are **of all men the most pitiable**."* (emphasis mine)

I would add, if only in the 70 years we exist on earth, we have hope in Christ and then die with nothing, we could only be considered the most foolish and ignorant people on earth! Paul is most definitely addressing those who have believed a lie that has been told them from another source other than Paul. The lie? There is no resurrection! Paul addresses the Corinthians who believe this lie in verses 33-34 AMP:

> *"Do not be so deceived and misled! Evil companionships (communion, associations) corrupt and deprave good manners and morals and character. Awake [from your drunken stupor and return] to sober sense and your right minds, and sin no more. For some of you have not the knowledge of God [you are utterly and willfully and disgracefully ignorant, and continue to be so, lacking the sense of God's presence and all true knowledge of Him]. I say this to your shame."*

We can see that the Corinthians have turned away from the faith they first believed in and Paul is a little upset. It's no wonder the Corinthians were concerned about their loved ones not being resurrected from the dead! They believed the lie! Paul goes on to address this lie with the truth in verses 51-52:

> *"Behold, I tell you a mystery: We shall not all sleep, but we shall all be changed---in a moment, in the twinkling of an eye, at the **last trumpet**.* (emphasis mine)

The mystery is not the rapture, but the fact that we will ALL (dead or alive) be changed at the last trumpet!

Many have endeavored to explain what the last trumpet means in Scripture. Some have said it is when the 7th trumpet judgment sounds. Others say it relates to the Feast of Trumpets or Rosh Hashana, which it is now called by modern day Jews. The Hebrew meaning for Rosh Hashana is "the head of months" or New Year.[3] (The web sight is given in the footnote in case you would like to study this on your own.) I believe the last trumpet could be associated with this feast, but I'm not dogmatic in this thought. The following will explain what I believe and why I believe it this way.

To begin explaining my belief of the last trumpet, I will begin in Exodus. Exodus 19 gives a picture or prelude of our encounter with Jesus when He returns. Moses prepares the people for their encounter by explaining to the children of Israel what will happen and how they are to prepare. He tells them when the trumpet sounds long, they are to come near the mountain. On the third day there were thunderings and lightnings and a thick cloud that encompassed the mountain. There was also the sound of a very loud trumpet. It then says that when the trumpet became louder and louder Moses spoke, and God answered him by voice. This is noteworthy: The loud trumpet and God's voice speaking coincide with each other. Let me explain. In 1 Thessalonians 4:13-15, we see a very similar situation unfolding as was with the Corinthians. There was concern over loved ones who had died before Jesus had returned and that they would not be resurrected.

> *"I do not want you to be ignorant, brethren, concerning those who have fallen asleep, lest you sorrow as others who have no hope. For if we believe that Jesus died and rose again, even so God will bring with Him those who sleep in Jesus. For this we say to you by the word of the Lord, that we who are alive and remain until the coming of the*

---

[3] https://www.levitt.com/essays/roshhashana/

> *Lord will by no means precede those who are asleep."*

We find the Thessalonians have given in to the same lie as did the Corinthians: There wasn't going to be a resurrection! Paul's expression of comfort in 1 Thessalonians 4:18 was not because of Jesus' return, but that God would bring with Him those who had died in Jesus. It goes on in verse 16 proclaiming:

> *"The Lord Himself will descend from heaven **with a shout, with the voice of an archangel**, and with the **trumpet** of God."* (emphasis mine)

Here we see, as in Exodus 19, a voice speaking along with a trumpet sound. It says the Lord will shout with the voice of an archangel! I don't know what an archangel sounds like when he speaks, but I do understand what a seraphim sounds like when he speaks! Isaiah 6:2-4 says:

> *"Seraphim . . . one cried to another . . . and **the posts of the door were shaken by the voice of him who cried out**."* (emphasis mine)

Shaken by a voice? That's one loud voice! The book of Revelation has several places mentioning angels speaking with loud voices; even those that sound like a lion roaring or thunder. However, the most important voice in Scripture is the voice of the Lord. John writes in Revelation 1:10:

> *"I was in the Spirit on the Lord's Day, and I heard behind me **a loud voice, as of a trumpet** . . . then **I turned to see the voice** that spoke with me. And having turned **I saw . . . One like the Son of Man**."* (emphasis mine)

John also hears this same trumpet voice saying, *"Come up here!"* and then he is caught up to heaven seeing a throne and One sitting on the throne (Revelation 4). The voice that Paul mentions in 1 Thessalonians 4:16 is the voice of Jesus. He shouts and sounds like an archangel. However, He didn't sound just like an archangel, but also like a trumpet. Here we see the dead in Christ rising first and then whoever is remaining alive will be caught up in the clouds to be with Jesus forever! Notice His voice calls and commands the dead to come to life.

Remember what Jesus said in Matthew 24:13:

"He who endures to the end shall be saved."

These will be those who are alive and remain as Paul says in 1 Thessalonians. His voice brings all believers to attention and calls them to Himself. The trumpet sound in Exodus 19 was the voice of Jesus calling Israel to Himself! When the trumpet became louder, God's voice spoke! Please notice Exodus 20:18-19:

> *"Now all the people witnessed the thunderings, the lightning flashes, the sound of the trumpet, and the mountain smoking; and when the people saw it, they trembled and stood afar off. Then they said to Moses, 'You speak to us, and we will hear, but **let not God speak with us, lest we die.**'"* (emphasis mine)

In the thundering and lightning and trumpet sound, they heard God speaking to them! It wasn't just thunder or a trumpet that they heard! They heard His voice speaking to them! Notice they were afraid and didn't respond. So what happened to all these who didn't respond? They died in the wilderness. This must serve as an example to us; we must learn to hear the voice of God speaking to us; otherwise, we have no relationship with Him and will die in the wilderness.

Let me point out a couple more Scriptures that correspond with what I have just shared. The first is in Revelation 1:7, where it says that every eye will see Him! I'm assuming that when it says "every" it means every. This happens when He comes back in the clouds just as the angels told the disciples in Acts 1:11:

> *"Men of Galilee, why do you stand gazing up into heaven? This same Jesus, who was taken up from*

> *you into heaven, will so come in like manner as you saw Him go into heaven."*

These angels just promised the disciples that Jesus would come back for them in the same way He just left! Please forgive me, but this does not speak of a rapture as in a separate appearance as some would say. He is not going to come the first time (rapture) and then come again a second time (the day of the Lord). When it says every eye will see Him, even those who have pierced Him, it means all men everywhere (believer and non-believer) will see Him.

This leads us to Matthew 24:30 and the very words of Jesus spoken on this subject.

> ***Then** the sign of the Son of Man will appear in heaven, and then all the tribes of the earth will mourn, and they will see the Son of Man coming on the clouds of heaven with power and great glory."*
> (Matthew 24:4-29 – emphasis mine)

The word "**Then**" refers to His appearing after all of the chaos happens. Jesus doesn't sugarcoat what He says in this chapter. He speaks it as it will happen before His return. After what He prophesies, He then says He will send His angels with a great sound of a trumpet (His voice) and they will gather together His elect from the four winds, from one end of heaven to the other. (Verse 31) I believe this is what is called in 1 Corinthians 15:52 "The last trumpet!" There will be no need for another trumpet to sound from this day on and forever! It is the "last" trumpet never to be heard by His people again! When we have sweet fellowship with Jesus; listening to Him speak to us in eternity, there will be no need for Him to get our attention. He will have it forever! When we are in our corruptible state as Paul describes in 1 Corinthians 15:52-53, we must be raised incorruptible. This will only happen when the last trumpet sounds; when Jesus shouts, "Come up here!" very loudly! Then the saying will be brought to pass, *"Death is swallowed up in victory!"* It's no wonder His voice will shout like an archangel and trumpet together. He's bringing the dead to life and they will never experience death ever again!!! He is very excited about this event and will not contain Himself because it was why He was crucified and resurrected. All this being said leads us back to my original question: What does I Corinthians 15:58 have to do with the last trumpet?

> *"Therefore, my beloved brethren, be steadfast, immovable always abounding in the work of the Lord..."*

If we are not resurrected, if this corruption doesn't put on incorruption, if we are not changed in the twinkling of an eye at the last trumpet, if death is not swallowed up in victory, then why bother being steadfast, immovable, always abounding in God's work?

GOD IS IN COMPLETE CONTROL AT ALL TIMES [Nothing is ever out of His control!]

January 12, 2017

*"Jesus answered Pilate, 'You could have no power at all against Me **unless it had been given you** from above.'"* (John 19:11 – emphasis mine)

    I need to be very careful as I expound on the following subject, for the reason that as it unfolds, it could cause someone to have an offense against God. We must remember that God is all in all! He knows all, sees all, perceives all, and is in all things---omniscient! Nothing escapes His watchful eyes. He gives power and authority to those on earth and also in heaven. I will endeavor to explain this as the chapter unfolds.

    Jesus stood before Pilate, having been accused by the religious leaders of blasphemy. Pilate was afraid of Jesus at this point since he had just heard from these leaders that Jesus made

Himself out to be the Son of God. In desperation, Pilate asked Jesus where He was from, of which Jesus remained silent. Pilate was taken back by this response and told Jesus that he alone had the power to release Him or to crucify Him. Jesus then makes an incredible statement (John 19:11) that would set the stage for God's purposes in the end times. Jesus basically said that **all power is granted by God**---even to wicked rulers so that His plan can be fulfilled! This is the very thing that we see proclaimed in 1Corithians 2:7-8:

> *"We speak the wisdom of God in a mystery, the hidden wisdom which God ordained before the ages for our glory, which none of the rulers of this age knew; for had they known, they would not have crucified the Lord of glory."*

It was God's purpose for His Son to be put to death and He would use the ungodly to fulfill His purposes; not just for salvation, but to destroy His enemies in the last days. Let me explain. In John's gospel we see that Jesus was troubled and He asked God to save Him from the hour that He was facing. He also knew that it was God's purpose and plan for Him to be crucified. Jesus then makes another incredible statement, in the light of His coming crucifixion, concerning the wicked ruler of darkness:

> *"Now is the judgment of this world;* ***now the ruler of this world will be cast out."*** (John 12:31 - emphasis mine)

Jesus knew that His obedience to God's plan would consume, destroy, and eradicate all evil from this earth, even though it would be implemented through the wicked.

Before I continue on this thought, I would like to expound further on God using wicked rulers to bring about His plan and purposes on earth. In Deuteronomy 28, we see the blessings and the curses upon Israel depending on how they would respond or not respond in obedience to God's voice. One of the curses that would come upon Israel for their disobedience was recorded in Deuteronomy 28:49-51:

> ***"The Lord will bring a nation against you from afar,*** *from the end of the earth, as swift as the eagle flies, a nation whose language you will not understand, a nation of fierce countenance, which does not respect the elderly nor show favor to the young. And they shall eat the increase of your livestock and the produce of your land, until you are destroyed; they shall not leave you grain or new wine or oil, or the increase of your cattle or the offspring of your flocks, until they have destroyed you."* (emphasis mine)

This curse was talking about the nation of Babylon and how Nebuchadezzar and the Chaldeans would come and completely destroy Israel's homes, livelihoods, families, and even their temple, which God had given them. Jeremiah had also expounded on and prophesied to them concerning this curse. He had warned them for several years leading up to the invasion of Babylon. When Babylon had broken through the walls of Jerusalem and occupied the city, we read that the Babylonian captain of the guard spoke these words to Jeremiah:

> ***"The Lord your God has pronounced this doom*** *on this place.* ***Now the Lord has brought it,*** *and has done just as He said,* ***because you people have sinned against the Lord****, and not obeyed His voice, therefore this thing has come upon you."* (Jeremiah 40:2-3 - emphasis mine)

Had the Babylonian captain of the guard been reading Deuteronomy 28? Out of the mouth of an ungodly ruler came the very thing the Lord had spoken many years earlier. This is something very serious to consider in regard to the United States. Are the blessings and curses only spoken for Israel's sake? Does a nation that overall claim to be Christian stand exempt of them? We as a nation are very quick to claim the blessings; yet we reject the curses claiming they come directly from Satan or, even worse, were only for Israel. We fail to recognize that God is holy and He will not go against His own Word. His word is forever settled in heaven and it pertains to everyone; believer and atheist, black and white, submissive and rebellious. In light of the curses, we need to understand that the coming of Babylon was prophesied by Moses (Deuteronomy 28:49-57) and that Daniel, through Nebuchadnezzar's dream (Daniel 2), prophesied the coming of another evil nation, the Roman Empire. Pilate was governor at this time and had the power of his position in the Roman Empire to crucify Jesus. Here we have two notoriously wicked nations being used by God to bring about His purposes in the earth. Pilate, who had Jesus crucified, was most likely unaware of a prophecy in Deuteronomy 21:22-23:

> *"If a man has committed a sin deserving of death, and he is put to death, and you hang him on a tree . . . he who is hanged is accursed of God."*

Paul visits this again in Galatians 3:13:

> *"Christ has redeemed us from the curse of the law, having become a curse for us for it is written, 'Cursed is everyone who hangs on a tree.'"*

I re-emphasize that God not only used Pilate, a Roman governor, but He also used white washed tombs, the scribes and Pharisees, (Matthew 23:27) to see that Jesus was crucified!

As I said earlier in this chapter, God also gives power and authority to those in the heavenly realms. Please let me explain. Paul, in the book of Ephesians, addresses Christians to put on the whole armor of God that we can stand against the strategies and the deceits of the devil. WHY?

> *"For we are not wrestling with flesh and blood [contending only with physical opponents], but against the despotisms, against the powers, against [the master spirits who are] the world rulers of this present darkness, against the spirit forces of wickedness in the heavenly (supernatural) sphere*
> (Ephesians 6:12 AMP).

The question arises: Do these spirit rulers have power and authority because they usurped it in their rebellion against God, or did God give it to them? I'd like to answer this with an earthly example from Genesis 16, where we find Abraham's wife, Sarah, treating Hagar the mother of Ishmael very harshly. Hagar ran from Abraham and Sarah and was confronted by an angel who told her to return and submit. The angel also prophesied over her and Ishmael:

> *"Behold, you are with child, and you shall bear a son. You shall call his name Ishmael, because the Lord has heard your affliction.* **He shall be a wild man; his hand shall be against every man**, *and every man's hand against him. And* **he shall dwell in the presence of all his brethren.** *"*
> (Genesis 16:11-12 – emphasis mine)

Ishmael has now become an Islamic nation that hates Israel and wants to completely destroy the Israelis as a nation! Ishmael is the son of Abraham; however, Abraham is also the grandfather of Jacob, who is Israel! Don't you think God knew this would happen in the future? I can't fail to mention Lot's grandkids, Ammon and Moab, who later became Islamic nations that also hate Israel. Before you call me an Islamophobe, I should mention that God is supernaturally appearing to Muslims and speaking directly to them about salvation in Jesus Christ. They are coming to Jesus in droves! The point I was making is that God allowed and even raised up these nations as an opposition to Israel, the apple of His eye! God did it! God allowed it!

I believe He does the same with the dark rulers in the heavenly places. Case in point: the tenth plague that came upon Egypt was the death of the first born of all Egyptians and their livestock. Israel was to slay a lamb and put its blood on the doorway of their houses. This was a sign to the Israelites that their firstborn children would be saved from death. Was it the Lord who put the Egyptian firstborn to death or did God allow something else to take their lives? We read in Exodus 12:23 the answer to this question:

> *"The Lord will pass through to strike the Egyptians; and when He sees the blood on the lintel and on the two doorposts, the Lord will pass over the door **and not allow the destroyer to come into your houses** to strike you."* (emphasis mine)

Who is this destroyer? We read in Revelation 9 about the fifth trumpet judgment and the angel who was the ruler or king over the stinging locusts. It speaks of him as a star fallen from heaven and that to him was given the key to the bottomless pit. In reading verse 11, we find out that his name is Abaddon (meaning destruction) and Apollyon (meaning Destroyer)! Revelation 20:2 calls him the dragon, that serpent of old, who is the Devil and Satan, and casts him into the bottomless pit for one thousand years before releasing him again to deceive the nations. As with the Destroyer in the death of the firstborn of Egypt and Apollyon who opened the bottomless pit, they were both allowed and given permission to do these things. Follow me to the book of Revelation for further explanation.

I will be pointing out several Scriptures throughout the book of Revelation and touching on this very thing. We must understand that God is in control always! He gives permission, but always has a future goal in mind, which is of utmost importance. This is the very reason John wept much when no one was found worthy to open the scroll. He knew that what was on the scroll was of utmost importance in the destiny of believers.

The first section of the book of Revelation that we will look at is the first five seals that are on the scroll (Revelation 6:1-11).

- The first seal is a rider on a white horse and it says a crown **was given** to him! He went out to conquer! Who gave him that crown?

- The second seal is a rider on a fiery red horse who takes peace from the earth and sets men against one another to kill one another. It says **this was granted** to him! It also says **he was given** a great sword! Who granted this? Who gave him this sword?

- The third seal is a rider on a black horse with a pair of scales in his hand. A voice spoke commanding **do not harm** the oil and wine. Who was behind the voice commanding this?

- The fourth seal was a rider on a pale horse whose name was Death and Hades followed him like a mangy, dirty, old, vicious dog! It says **power was given** them! Who gave them this power?

- The fifth seal are slain souls under the altar. They are slain because of the Word of God and their testimony. We know that these are dear to the heart of God, so we must conclude that when it says a **white robe was given to them and that they were to rest** a little while longer, that it was God, their Father, who spoke this comfort to them! God is in control at all times! He knows what the end will look like!

The second section ranges between Revelation 7 and 9.
- In chapter 7, we see four angels bent on destruction. They were **commanded to not harm** until all Jews were sealed (144,000). Again, we see these angels **had been granted** the ability to harm the earth and sea. Who granted this to them?

- In chapter 9:1-12, we see stinging locusts and **power was given to them** to torment men that do not have the seal of God on their foreheads. These locusts **were also commanded** not to eat any green thing and they were **not given authority** to kill, but only to torment! Again, who is commanding and giving the authority to these locusts?

- In chapter 9:14, we hear the command "... *Release the four angels ...!*" (emphasis mine) Verse 15 says that these four angels **had been prepared** for their mission. It took a few years, months, days and hours for them to be prepared and **then they were released to kill**. We see clearly from verse 13 that the voice who directed these angels came from the four horns of the golden altar. Whose voice could it have been other than God's? The Lord spoke these words! God is in control at ALL times!!!

The third section is chapter 11.
- Verse 2 says that the court of the temple **had been given** to the Gentiles. Who gave this to them?

- Verse 3 says that **power was given** to the two witnesses so they could prophesy for three and one-half years. Who gave this power to them? I'm sure you know the answer to this question.

- At the end of these years of prophecy, the Beast kills the two witnesses, not allowing them to be buried. They lay dead in the streets of Jerusalem for three and one-half days while their enemies rejoice and send gifts to each other. After the three and one-half days, they hear a voice from heaven saying: *"Come up here!"* They went to heaven immediately! Again, we see that God is the One who gave the final command! (Revelation 11:8, 10, 12)

The last section I would like to expound on is in Revelation 12 and 13.
- In chapter 12 we see two elements: A woman and a dragon. The woman is a sign or representation of saved Israel. She is clothed with the sun, the moon is under her feet, and she has twelve stars on her head. She is pregnant and gives birth to a male Child who is caught up to heaven. It's this Child who will be ruling all nations! The dragon endeavors to devour the Child, but is unsuccessful since this Child is caught up to God and seated on His throne. The Child is Jesus! The woman (saved Israel) then flees to a place **prepared for her by God**. So we see God in control of all things once again!

- I believe that the dragon or Satan is completely controlled by God at this point. It might look as though all hell has broken out on the earth; yet God is working through His people as they overcame by the blood of the Lamb, testify with their words about God, and are willing to die for Jesus, not loving their own lives!!! God and His obedient people Israel are bringing about the demise of the Devil! Revelation 12:7 says war broke out in heaven. Two sets of angels were engaged in conflict; Michael and his angels and Satan and his angels. Satan did not prevail! This is where it gets exciting! IT SAYS THERE WAS **NO PLACE IN HEAVEN** ANY LONGER FOR SATAN AND HIS ANGELS!!! They were all cast out of heaven, both Satan and his angels forever! Even though this is a tremendous victory the story isn't over yet. Satan was cast to the earth along with his angels. This is where we enter chapter 13.

- Revelation 13:1 says that John saw the first beast with seven heads and ten horns with ten crowns upon them. On the seven heads a blasphemous name! It's clear in verse 2 who gave the power, throne, and authority to the beast; THE DRAGON (Satan)! It's not clear who gave the beast his mouth and the authority to continue his rampage for three and one-half years. Just the fact that he was **given a mouth** means he was given the authority to speak with a voice! Then in verse 7, we must ask the question who **granted to him the power to make war with the saints and to overcome them**? Who **gave to him authority** over every person on earth? This is something that we just cannot overlook, but must be careful to understand. Things are not out of control for God! He is in control!

- Then there is a second beast (verse 11) that seems to always be in the presence and in the sight of the first beast. Don't you find this unusual language: phrases like "in his presence" and "in his sight"? It's mentioned of the second beast that **he was granted** to do incredible signs and wonders in the sight and presence of the first beast in order to deceive people. It also says **he was granted** power to give breath to an image of the first beast. Breath was given in order to have the power of a voice so that it could speak and that those who don't worship will be put to death. Colossians 1:15 says that Jesus is the image of the invisible God and He gives life to those who believe! So what is this image that is made in the likeness of the first beast? We must remember that God is in control no matter what it looks like. It says in Revelation 14:9 that the wine of the wrath of God will be poured out on anyone who worships the beast and **his image** (which could possibly be his nature and being---as God Himself has an image of His nature and being Genesis 1:27). God has all things in control and will bring His kingdom to fullness, but it will be at His pace of which we get very impatient.

Yes, we get very impatient with God sometimes because we think He's too slow!! Many people don't watch for His return because they think He is too slow. So they fill their lives with what I call "blessing band aids". These would be promise Scriptures, books, prophecies, music, etc. that bring good feelings to the soul, but don't address the times we live in. They are not willing to take a good hard look at what Jesus called the signs of the times as in the parable of the fig tree (Matthew 24:32-35). He said when you see these things begin to happen know that He is right at the door! We can be assured that God has everything in the palm of His hand and is methodically bringing the eradication of evil and establishing the all-consuming power of His kingdom forever!

In this chapter, we have seen how God "gives and grants" power just as He did with Satan when testing Job. On the other hand, He has granted and given power to us too, as His people. This is seen throughout the pages of history just as we see what happens with Job's life after his test. God restored to Job twice as much as he had before. Yes, God gives to His people power for life and godliness, for prosperity and favor, and the ability to overcome every obstacle and sin in this life.

I hope your getting what I've been trying to communicate since it is vital to the understanding of the revelation within the Book of Revelation. This book is not information, it's revelation: living, breathing, vitally active, always on the move in order to conquer and consume for God and His glory! This Revelation is not just the evil that will come on this world, but of the very revelation of Jesus Christ for and in His people! God has all things under control!

There is a reason why Jesus declares His sovereignty two times in the first chapter of Revelation: *"**I am the Alpha and the Omega, the Beginning and the End**," says the Lord, "**who is and who was and who is to come, the Almighty**."* (emphasis mine) He is establishing that all things are subject to His authority. Nothing will be overlooked.

> The twenty-four elders also see this and proclaim:
> ***"You are worthy, O Lord, to receive glory and honor and power; for You created all things, and by Your will they exist and were created."*** (emphasis mine)

> All of the angels are proclaiming with loud voices:
> ***"Worthy is the Lamb who was slain to receive power and riches and wisdom, and strength and honor and glory and blessing!"***
> (emphasis mine)

Every creature in heaven, in earth, under the earth and also in the sea are proclaiming:
> ***"Blessing and honor and glory and power be to Him who sits on the throne, and to the Lamb forever and ever!"*** (emphasis mine)

I believe this next proclamation by the four living creatures and the twenty-four elders is overlooked and not taken seriously by many a believer:
> ***"You are worthy to take the scroll, and to open its seals; for You were slain, and have redeemed us to God by Your blood out of every tribe and tongue and people and nation, and have made us kings and priests to our God; and we shall reign on the earth."*** (emphasis mine) Do you know that we will be reigning on the earth?

Angels know whom they serve, but humans live in fear and intimidation because of a lack of faith and simple trust in God. Notice what this angel proclaims in Revelation 10:5-6:

> *"The angel whom I saw standing on the sea and on the land **raised up his hand to heaven and swore by Him who lives forever and ever, who created heaven and the things that are in it, the earth and the things that are in it, and the sea and the things that are in it . . ."*** (emphasis mine)

Would we live in fear if we knew and completely understood that God created all things everywhere? Nothing is overlooked! Nothing exists without His knowledge of it! Everything exists for His will and purposes to be accomplished in heaven and in earth! He has never said, "Oops, I didn't see that one coming!"

We must believe what Colossians 1:16-17 AMP proclaims:

> *"For it was in Him that all things were created, in heaven and on earth, things seen and things unseen, whether thrones, dominions, rulers, or authorities; all things were created and exist through Him [by His service, intervention] and in and for Him. And He Himself existed before all things, and in Him all things consist (cohere, are held together)."*

Believe and be blessed forever!

www.ingramcontent.com/pod-product-compliance
Lightning Source LLC
Chambersburg PA
CBHW061330040426
42444CB00011B/2854